"Diana Greene's book of prayer parables is a delightful journey that will take the reflective reader deep into prayer, the life blood of our relation with Jesus. Drink deeply and grow."

Gerry Breshears, PhD
Professor of Theology
Western Seminary, Portland
Co-Author of *Death by Love*

"Unplug our ears, Lord. We long to hear Your voice. Use Diana Greene's book to pole vault our prayers from mediocre monologues to dialogues with the Divine."

Judy Squier
Speaker
Author of *His Majesty in Brokenness*

"Diana Greene's journey with the Lord draws you into a desire for more: more listening, more attending, and more awareness of how close our Lord Jesus really is to each of us. Take time to let the water soak into your soul. Drink deep. Remain in his presence. He really does care for you. You can't miss that message in *Where is the Water?*"

Bev Hislop, D.Min.
Assoc. Professor of Pastoral Care to Women
Western Seminary, Portland
Author of *Shepherding a Woman's Heart*

Where is the Water?

Judy,

Thank you for all you do to put food on our table!

Diana

Finding the Extraordinary in the Ordinary

Diana E. Greene

Diana Greene Ministries, LLC

Copyright ©2012 by Diana E. Greene

All rights reserved. No part of this publication or any part thereof, may be reproduced, stored in a retrieval system, or transmitted in any form or by any means—electronic, mechanical, photocopy, recording, or any other—except for brief quotations in printed reviews, without the prior permission of the author except as provided by USA Copyright law.

Cover Photo by Bill Barth Copyright ©2005 Photography by Bill Barth. Copyright ©2001-3 All rights reserved.
Cover Design by Ruth Greene
Copyright ©2012 by Diana E. Greene. All rights reserved.

Layout by elabret designs www.elabret.com

Scripture quotations taken from the Holy Bible, Today's Parallel Bible, Copyright ©2000 Zondervan, Grand Rapids, Michigan 49530. Used by permission of Zondervan. All rights reserved worldwide.
www.zondervan.com

Scripture quotations taken from THE MESSAGE: The Bible in Contemporary Language, Copyright ©1993, 1995, 2000, 2001, 2002. Used by permission of NavPress Publishing Group. All rights reserved.

Published by Diana Greene Ministries, LLC, PO Box 902, Molalla, OR 97038 *www.DianaGreeneMinistries.com*

Library of Congress Cataloging-in-Publication Data

Greene, Diana E.
Where is the water? finding the extraordinary in the ordinary /by Diana E. Greene

ISBN-13: 978 - 1470130459
ISBN - 10: 1470130459

1. Inspirational 2. Prayer–Christian 3. Holy Spirit

Printed in the United States of America

To My Sons Luke and Nathan

Growing with you has been my greatest joy.

To My Husband John

Life with you has been an adventure.
Thank you for the memories—I love you.

Contents

Preface xi
Appreciation xiii
Introduction 17

Make Me 21
The Faith of a Five-Year-Old 25
Do Your Best and Let God Do the Rest 31
We Can't Eat All That 37
Nobody Loves Me 43
1, 2, 3—Go 49
If He Was Your Son, What Would You Do? 55
Are You Alright? 63
Do As I Tell You 67
Do You Really Want to Know? 71
Okay, You Lead and I Will Follow 79
Thought You Were an Angel 89
Tell Her She's Beautiful 97
I'm Going on a Cruise 105
If You Wait, It Will Be Too Late 113
Do You Have a Few Minutes? 121
You Can Go Deeper 127
Dialogue: Where is the Water? 135

Suggested Resources for Growth 146

Preface

When Moses encountered God he was tending sheep (Exodus 3 and 4). A woman met Jesus as she did the daily job of drawing water from a well (John 4). Saul, had no idea his life was about to change when he met the risen Christ on his way to Damascus. (Acts 9). For each person, God appeared while they were performing their daily tasks.

In my journals, I have recorded my stories of encountering God. Every story is based on true events collected over a lifetime. They weave a tapestry of: doubt, disappointment, fear, faith, trust, hope, grace, obedience and a willingness to risk. They relate experiences of learning how to pray. They reveal the extraordinary in the ordinary. After each story I have a reflection and a challenge.

In Reflection – *tells you* what I learned from God reaching out.

The Challenge – invites you to discern how to stop, look, listen and take action.

God's methods have not changed. He desires to be known. He touches you when you least expect him. He invites you to follow his plan.

Once you do, you are transformed. You see with new eyes, you hear with new ears. God is as close as your next breath. Invite him to join you in your daily life.

Preface

What he has done for me he can do for you. Believe you are a child of his. He loves you. He desires to give you his wisdom and power. He wants to change your ordinary day into an extraordinary one.

Like the woman at the well, ask him for the streams of living water.

> *"Sir, give me this water, so I will not be thirsty, nor come all the way here to draw."*
>
> John 4:15

> *"Whoever believes in me, as the Scripture has said, streams of living water will flow from within him."*
>
> John 7:38

Appreciation

The Lord chose people who do not know each other, who do not live in the same city, state or country to complete this project. The wonder of the internet, cell phones and Skype made it possible. I want to thank all who gave their time, talent and prayers.

Friendships that have the courage to disclose unmasked feelings take a lifetime to develop. Marcia Evans, your relationship with God, your insight into yourself and me, gave you the ability to give honest feedback. You have helped me grow as an author. It is you who have lived these stories with me. Thank you for agreeing to edit and relive them. I treasure our friendship.

The Lord blessed our team with a young woman who has a maturity way beyond her years. Amanda Halvorson, I understand why you have taken 1 Timothy 4:12 as your life verse. Your ability to edit and ask questions caused me to stand back, examine the stories for clarity and avoid a wall of words.

Denise LaMarsh, I am indebted to the long hours you devoted to this book. Your willingness to grow and to try something new blossomed the gifts God has given you. It was a joy to watch.

Appreciation

When my computer crashed and needed security protection the Lord provided David Wallace. I appreciate your extensive knowledge and generosity.

The front cover takes my breath away. Bill Barth, you have captured God's beauty through your gift of photography. I see the cross and the risen Christ above the water, revealed in the sunset. You were right—the wheat, water, and the cross create an awesome picture. The Lord has blessed you with his eye for nature's beauty. I love all the interior water pictures.

Ruth Greene, my precious daughter (in-law), I thank God for your artistic flair and your sweet spirit in sharing them. The cover and the cropping of the interior pictures are fantastic!

Some people are blessed with an eye for detail and making sure the overall product fits together—Gail Barth, I am so glad you were willing to share your talent.

Elizabeth Wallace, thank you for sharing your seminary training and English skills with us.

Luke Greene and Nathan Greene, I am grateful that amidst busy schedules you created time to proofread stories for accuracy and detail. I enjoyed reliving your growing years. You have become men who display generosity, kindness, grace and compassion. May the Lord's heart continue to grow in you.

Where is the Water?

John Greene, can you believe that after this many years *Where is the Water?* has become a reality? Your encouragement, patience, listening ear and reminder to "keep going, stay focused and listen to the Lord" gave me the momentum I needed to finish this lifelong dream.

Mom, thank you for your belief that "You can do it!" Your willingness to share your resources took this project from the drafting table to reality.

Thank you to everyone who prayed for our team. We all appreciate your prayers.

We serve an awesome God. He guided our work, brought who we needed exactly when we needed them and provided the means to complete this project.

Lord, thank you for your vision, faithfulness and love. I am grateful that you showed me, *Where is the Water?* I pray that your Holy Spirit continues to flow through my life and the lives of those who surrender to you.

Introduction

Do you ever wonder, "Where is God? You may have read amazing stories in Scripture or heard fantastic reports of people who have encountered God, but the events are hard to believe. Why? Could it be because you have yet to know the hope of God's presence?

I came to that point in my life. I was thirty-four, married with two small children. Life seemed to be one struggle after another. Then the extraordinary happened. God reached out and revealed himself in the everyday events of my life. My circumstances did not change, but my perception and my attitude did. Hearing the world around me with new ears and being invited to see the world with new eyes opened me to a life of hope. I realized God was not just a power that lived in the heavens. He was the strength and wisdom I could rely on every day.

I must confess I can be stubborn, hard headed, and demand that I know what is best, but God is patient. He waits until I have come to the end of myself and I am ready to do it his way.

He desires to teach me something new. My desire is to keep myself safe. When I allow him to pry me loose from what I already know, when I decide to trust him in the places that look dark and scary, I enter a whole new place of being.

Introduction

It is a place of courage that requires the ability to risk. In those places God promises his wisdom and strength. As long as I am willing to call on him, the reward is an intimate relationship with God. It is a life of receiving his grace. It is a life of adventure.

His grace allows me to see and hear. Once you see, once you hear, I promise that you will never go back to your old life.

If you have experienced years of silence it is time to renew your confidence in God. It is time to discover *Where is the Water?*

> *"Come!" say the Spirit and the Bride. Whoever Hears, echo, "Come!" Is anyone thirsty? Come! All who will, come and drink, Drink freely of the Water of Life!"*

Revelations 22:17

Diana E. Greene
Molalla, Oregon
Spring 2012

Make Me

Doors slammed shut and locked behind us, as we entered the fifteen bed dormitory. I began to unload my gear into a nearby locker. Suddenly, I felt the bottom of my sweater yanked up over my head. Like a smothering blanket wrapped around my face, it blocked my vision. I didn't fight. I could hear my attacker laughing. She discovered I was braless and released her grip. I pulled my sweater down from my head.

Thirty girls enveloped me, chattering in anticipation. A nineteen year old pushed herself forward from the back of the group, thrust a razor blade to my neck and held it there. I sucked in my breath and silently prayed,

"Jesus, be with me."

Motionless, I looked my aggressor straight in the eye. Screaming, she hurled threats at me, but my ears could not hear. I saw her lips moving, her face full of rage and her eyes wild with excitement. My heart was pounding in my throat. My mind was fumbling for words somewhere inside me. Without accusation, I asked her:

"Where'd you get that?"

I was surprised by the dominant strength in my voice not a hint of the panic in me.

"From one of the lockers," came her flippant reply.

"Well, put it back," I said calmly.

Her eyes dropped. Her hideous smile broadened, as she moved the razor closer to my neck. Her gaze came back to mine, as if to say,

Make me!

I never flinched. I never moved. I never broke my authoritative stare into those scornful eyes. I did not feel hate for her, but a strange mixture of pity and bewilderment. After all, I didn't even know this girl.

What had I done to evoke such loathing? Why did she feel the need to lash out at me? I had done nothing to her. I didn't even know her name.

I don't know how long we stood there. Our eyes fixed, looking into the depths of the other, expecting they'd give some kind of answer. Ultimately, she dropped her hand. I did not relax. Her shoulders rounded. She turned away and melted into the mob. I could hear her friends prodding her, but she exclaimed,

"Nah, let's forget it!"

I stood there rooted, watching them walk away. One young thirteen year old, who had been hiding from all the commotion, jumped onto the bed behind me and exclaimed,

"I'm staying with you tonight!"

In Reflection

When the razor blade incident happened, I was finishing my sophomore year of college as a counselor's helper at an all girls' juvenile delinquent school. I had just given my life to Christ the summer before and was learning the power of prayer.

Looking back, it is obvious to me that my aggressor had me. Not only that, she had thirty others to back her up! Yet, I went unharmed throughout the weekend. This event taught me that it is not the eloquence or length of my prayer that matters. What matters is that I call on him with the expectation that he will answer. I realize now there was a spiritual battle going on. There was an invisible armor surrounding me, keeping me protected.

The Challenge

Have you ever had something happen to you that defied explanation? Have you ever experienced the invisible armor of God?

A simple prayer as a child of God can protect you and move mountains. Believe the truth that you are adopted, that you are loved.

Make Me

What risk can you take while stepping out in faith? How can you develop an ear to do what is right in the heat of the battle?

Start by applying the power of prayer to your every day life, so when the wicked attack you are ready, armored and well protected.

∞ Further Study ∞

"Give ear to my prayer, O God; ... Because of the pressure of the wicked; For they bring down trouble upon me, And in anger they bear a grudge against me."

Psalm 55:1-3

"... everything you ask in prayer, believing, you shall receive."

Matthew 21:21-22

"Be strong with the Lord's mighty power. Put on all of God's armor so that you will be able to stand firm against the strategies and tricks of the Devil. For we are not fighting against people made of flesh and blood, but against the evil rulers and authorities of the unseen world, against those mighty powers of darkness who rule this world..."

Ephesians 6:10-13

The Faith of a Five-Year-Old

The sun was peeking through the trees on a glorious spring day. We had a birthday party to go to. As my sons, two and five, were busy wrapping their gifts the phone rang:

"We just came from the doctor." It was my best friend. "Ryan has pink eye."

"Oh, no!"

"The doctor says it's highly contagious, so we have to cancel the party."

"What?"

"I wanted to catch you before you drove all the way into town. Everyone is dropping off their presents and leaving. You don't have to come into town."

"We have the gifts wrapped. We're bringing them."

When I got off the phone I explained to Luke and Nathan:

"Ryan has pink eye. We'll go into town and drop off his presents. You can decide if you want to stay."

The Faith of a Five-Year-Old

"Pink eye is highly contagious," I continued, "like poison oak." Living in the woods, the boys knew how miserable poison oak was.

"It's up to you. I feel for Ryan. What would it be like if your birthday party was all set and no one came? Everyone has left presents, but big deal! What's a birthday party without friends to celebrate?"

It was quiet in the cab of the truck as we drove into town. Two blocks from Ryan's house Luke, sitting in his booster seat, commanded:

"Mom, pull the truck over."

"What?"

"Pull the truck over right here. I want to pray."

I pulled the truck over.

"What are you talking about?"

In response, Luke bowed his head and began to pray:

"Jesus, Ryan doesn't have anyone to go to his birthday party 'cuz he has the pink eye. Please protect us from the pink eye, while we go to his birthday party."

"Okay, Mom, let's go."

Oh, boy! How do I explain to my son that pink eye is highly contagious?

"Luke..."

"Mom, Jesus will protect us."

Where is the Water?

I didn't want to daunt the faith of my five year old, but I knew how pink eye could spread. On his faith I prayed silently,

"Lord, this would be a good time to increase Luke's faith in you!"

When we reached Ryan's front door, my friend greeted us. "Thanks for the presents. I can't believe you drove all the way into town to deliver them."

"We're coming in," I said, as I pushed passed her with the boys on my heels.

"What?"

"Luke prayed," was all I said. "We're staying."

She looked at me like, *Are you crazy?*

I shrugged my shoulders and nodded at the boys, already geared up for birthday party excitement.

We stayed all day. The boys ran in and out of the bathroom using the same towels. They sat at the grand birthday table my friend had prepared and had the time of their lives.

We never got pink eye. Two weeks later when one of our friends called to cancel a play date, because of pink eye, I boldly said,

"Oh, we don't get it. We're immune."

We went to the play date. And you guessed it! We all had the worst case of pink eye.

"Mom, we didn't pray."
"I know Luke. I know."

In Reflection

The faith of a five-year-old is what I need. To believe, to trust, that no matter what the circumstances or what other people are doing, Jesus will protect me and keep me safe. I have to remember to stop, to ask him for his protection and then listen for his reply. I have to be humble enough to realize within myself I do not have the ability to control the circumstances in my life. I do not have the strength, but with him *"all things are possible."* (Matthew 19:26)

The Challenge

Where in your life do you need the faith of a five-year-old to believe Jesus cares—even about the little things? He is just waiting for you to ask for his strength, his power.

Do you have faith to trust Jesus with your circumstances? Your family? Your work? Do you stop what you are doing, take time to pray and listen for his reply—or do you worry instead? If you worry, how can you change your worry habit into prayer time with God?

∞ Further Study ∞

"... I say to you, if you have faith as a mustard seed, you shall say to this mountain, 'Move from here to there, and it shall move; and nothing shall be impossible to you.'"

Matthew 17:20-21

"Mark my words, no one who sacrifices house, brothers, sister, mother, father, children, land—whatever—because of me and the Message will lose out. They'll get it all back, but multiplied many times ... but also in troubles. And then the bonus of eternal life! This is once again the Great Reversal: Many who are first will end up last, and the last first."

Mark 10:29-30

"And He has said to me, "My grace is sufficient for you, for power is perfected in weakness."

2 Corinthians 12:9

Do Your Best and Let God Do the Rest

One fall morning the house was unusually quiet, so I began an investigation to find out the reason. Peeking around the corner I spied my four-year-old son in his bedroom.

He stood atop his mattress precariously balanced at the foot of the bed. A crumpled blanket and sheet were around his feet. I watched as he bent over to grab folds of the top sheet. He walked backwards toward his pillow pulling the sheet with him.

He climbed off the bed and began pulling the sheet up a little more toward the pillow. When he was satisfied that he had pulled the sheet as far as it would go, he climbed back onto the bed to retrieve the blanket.

As I remained incognito, he started the process all over again walking backwards toward the head of the bed, blanket in hand. He again climbed off the bed pulling the blanket the rest of the way to the pillow. He proceeded to do the same with the bedspread.

Do Your Best and Let God Do the Rest

As he stood back to survey his bed, he was not satisfied. He tried to smooth the covers. When they refused to move he began pounding the lumps! Once again he stood back to survey his work. Hands on his hips he shook his head in disgust. He tried again to flatten the covers by climbing back on the bed and pulling them all together toward the pillow.

His face was scrunched in dissatisfaction. As he climbed back down, I scurried to the kitchen and hurriedly busied myself with sudsy dishes. In he came:

"Mom!"

"In here, Nathan."

"Mom, Psalty (a singing song book for children) says, "Do your best and let God do the rest.""

"Yes, that's right."

In utter frustration he declared,

"Then how come there are still lumps in my bed?!"

In Reflection

Watching Nathan I realized sometimes despite my best efforts things do not turn out quite like I expect. Often it is because I expect perfection. God expects effort.

His and my perceptions of "perfect" are not always the same. The continuing development of my character requires growth. Growth requires being willing to make mistakes, hammer out the lumps and try again. God promises to help me in the transformation process. He delights in watching me, his child, grow.

The Challenge

What new adventure have you been avoiding because you were afraid you would not be able to do it perfectly?

Study someone you admire. Someone you consider successful. How many years of trial and error did it take for them to reach their current success? How many times did they not give up?

If you have tried and failed—try again. Only this time call for reinforcements. God has a plan for your life. With the gifts he gave you, he plans for you to succeed. Ask him his intention. Ask him for the first step toward his dream for you.

Do Your Best and Let God Do the Rest

Remember God does not expect perfection. Watch out that you do not harbor an attitude of defeat or give up because you hold yourself to unrealistic expectations. Ask yourself, *Am I willing to do my best and let God do the rest?*

Believe God is proud of the job you did "making the bed." He wants you to trust him to do the rest.

Trust him that what you did with the time and resources you had was enough, even though you see the lumps. He does not call us to be perfectionists, but to be obedient and holy, as he is holy.

What new adventure with God are you ready to tackle today?

∞ Further Study ∞

"Trust in the Lord with all your heart, and do not lean on your own understanding; in all your ways acknowledge Him, and He will make your paths straight."

Proverbs 3:5-6

"I can do all things through Him who strengthens me."

Philippians 4:13

We Can't Eat All That

"Good Friday is tomorrow. Your parents will be here this afternoon. What am I going to feed them for dinner on Friday?"

John, my husband, was getting ready to head out the door for work. I wanted help getting what I needed for the weekend menu.

"I don't know. You'll think of something."

"Your mother is going to expect fish for Good Friday. Where am I going to get fish?"

"I don't know. I've gotta go. I'll see you tonight."

"I'll pray about it. I don't know what else to do," I added.

John gave me a quick "good bye" kiss and left. I sat down to pray before the boys got up for breakfast.

In the afternoon John's folks arrived. His mom opened the fridge to put the few things from their cooler in it. She stopped short when she found there was plenty of room to put away their groceries. The refrigerator was almost empty. Turning toward me she asked:

We Can't Eat All That

"What did you plan to have for dinner?"

"I don't know. I haven't figured it out yet."

There was a pot of beans on the wood stove for Thursday night, but I knew she was talking about Good Friday. Sitting around the dining room table we managed to avoid the topic, until John burst through the back door.

He was carrying a large green garbage bag over his right shoulder. He didn't bother with the formalities of greeting everyone. Instead he looked directly at his mother and said,

"I want you to know Diana prayed."

She was stunned with his first words. He had her attention.

"She did not know what to feed you for Good Friday. She knew that you would expect fish, but we didn't have any, so she prayed."

As he was talking, he flopped the garbage bag onto the table, took his knife out of his pocket and ripped open the bag. There was a gigantic Chinook salmon.

"We can't eat all that!" was her first reply.

"Where'd you get the fish, Son?" his dad inquired.

"Well, I'll tell 'ya. I had a patio to put in for a guy today. He and a couple of his buddies went salmon fishing. They each caught their limit. When he got home he said he had three big salmon. His freezer was already full of fish. He couldn't eat it all. He wanted to know if I'd take one."

"Wow! That's a lot of fish," he exclaimed.

Where is the Water?

John's dad had commercial fished a couple of summers. He was standing over the table admiring the size of the Chinook.

I couldn't believe it. There was our Good Friday dinner and then some!! I gave John a kiss on the cheek and he turned to give me a big hug. Then he looked at me with a wide grin and said,

"The Lord answered your prayer."

He looked at the salmon and then back at me. He gave me another hug.

In Reflection

Believing God for the impossible had become a way of life while living in the backwoods of our fifty-two acre tree farm. Time and time again, God answered our prayers. I was learning to pray about everything. Looking back I realize it wasn't so much about meeting our needs or satisfying our hunger for food as it was about building our faith in him.

The Challenge

Has the God of the impossible come through for you? If not yet, what do you need to believe about God?

He says he will give us the desire of our hearts. That does not mean he is going to be your Santa Claus or your "go-to" guy. It means when you pray *his* heart, *his* desires for you and believe without a doubt that he will answer—he will.

It takes diligent prayer. It takes being willing not to go ahead of the Spirit. What does that mean?

Be still, be patient and wait on God's Spirit instead of taking matters into your own hands.

Pray. Stay alert. Take time to listen.

When you get an answer, ask God for the plan to move toward his will one step at a time.

Go in confidence that God knows where he is leading you. Believe he is faithful. He loves you.

What impossible request can you ask God for today?

∞ Further Study ∞

"Delight yourself in the LORD and he will give you the desires of our heart."

Psalm 37:4

Where is the Water?

"Listen, God—I'm desperate. Don't be too busy to hear me..."

Psalm 54:2

"...For my house will be called a house of prayer for all the nations."

Isaiah 56:7

"Ask and it will be given to you; seek and you will find; knock and the door will be opened to you. For everyone who asks receives; he who seeks finds; and to him who knocks, the door will be opened. Which of you, if his son asks for bread, will give him a stone? Or if he asks for a fish, will give him a snake? If you then, though you are evil, know how to give good gifts to your children, how much more will your Father in heaven give good gifts to those who ask him!"

Matthew 7:7-11

" ... whenever trouble comes your way, let it be an opportunity for joy. For when your faith is tested, your endurance has a chance to grow... If you need wisdom...ask him...But when you ask, be sure you really expect him to answer for a doubtful mind is as unsettled as the wave of the sea that is driven and tossed by the wind."

James 1:2-5

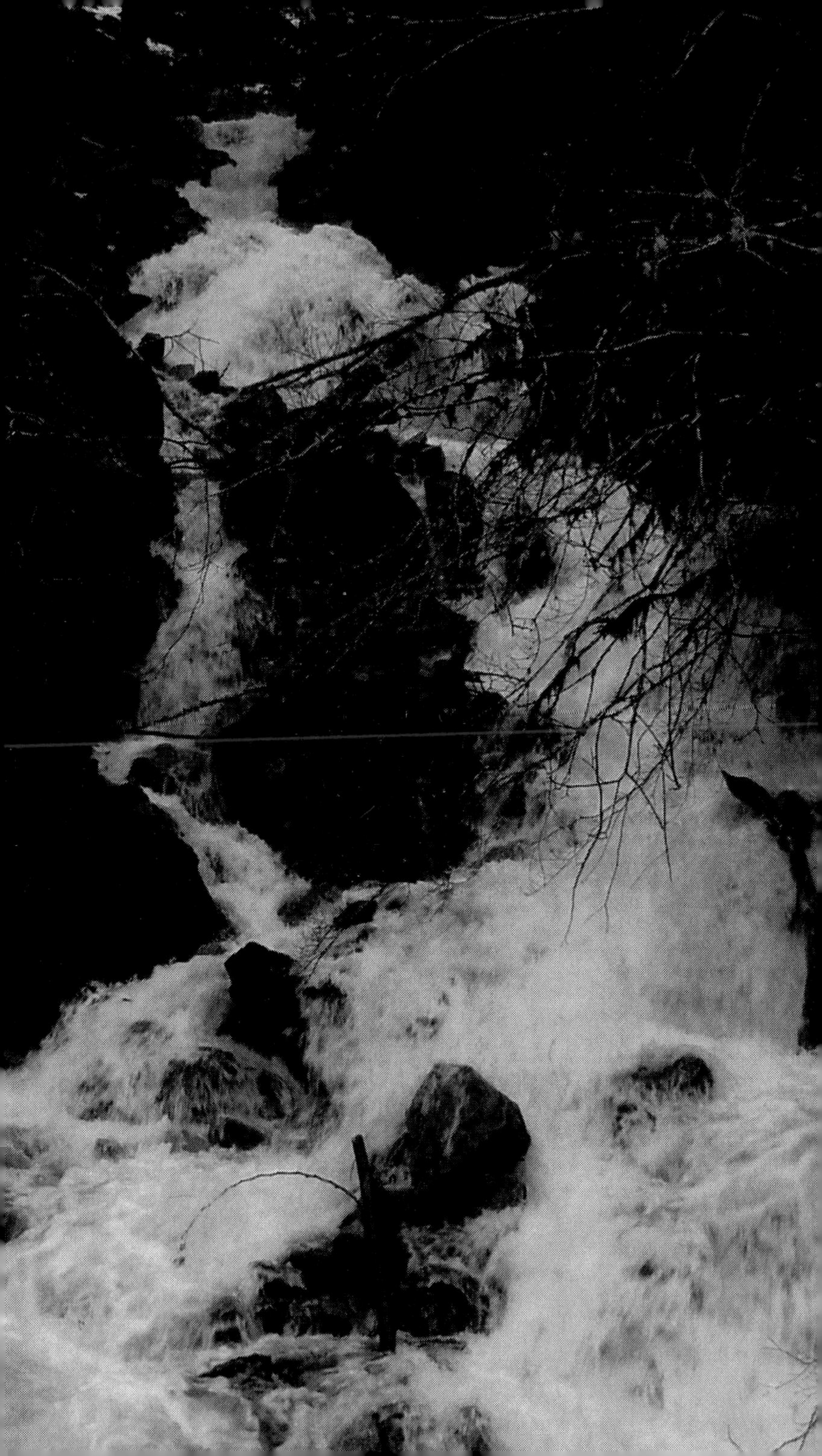

Nobody Loves Me

When we bought our fifty-two acres we dreamed of having a Labrador to run on the property. John couldn't believe I was praying and asking the Lord for just the right dog. He said:

"That's so stupid. He doesn't care what kind of dog you get. Why don't you save your prayers for big things like...?"

"This could be a big thing. I've never had a dog, but I've heard they can be a real pain. You want a dog that barks all the time? Or tears things up? Besides you want a Lab don't you? Well, we can't afford a Lab, but the Lord will find us one."

"Well, do what you like, but I still think it's a silly idea."

I prayed, "*Lord, please find us the right Lab, one that doesn't bark a lot and would be a good family dog. I know you know all the trouble a dog could be. I don't, so would you help us pick out a dog?*"

Nobody Loves Me

A few weeks later, I had an urge to call the dog shelter to see if they had a Lab. They said,

"Well, as a matter of fact we do. We don't get them in very often. We usually get mutts. A lady brought in a full blooded Lab a couple of days ago; said she couldn't sell it because its back teeth didn't come in. Anyway, she's seven months old. We also have some six week old puppies that are part Lab if you want to come take a look. We can only keep them two weeks. I sure hate to destroy that Lab though."

When John came home we headed for the pound. The man showed us the seven month old dog first. She looked full grown to me, not exactly what I had in mind.

"She's been cowering back in that cage since they brought her; doesn't seem to care for men much. She acts like she's been abused." The keeper told us.

Her sad eyes looked up at us and she took my heart.

"The pups are over here."

He took us around to the other side of the cage. What a difference. They were so lively and friendly. He let a couple of them out of the cage. Our son was two-years-old. They ran with him, jumped up on him and bit at his feet. He laughed with joy. He loved the puppies.

"They're full of it aren't they. They're so cute. We won't have any trouble getting rid of them." The attendant informed us.

"What about the older dog?" I asked.

"Well, it's harder getting rid of a full grown dog. We only have two weeks, but she's a full blooded Lab so someone's bound to take her."

John and I walked back around to her cage. She cowered and gave us this forlorn look as if to say,

Nobody loves me. We melted.

"So what do you think?" I asked John.

"I don't know. You're the one who prayed."

"Well, the puppies are cute, but they're going to take a lot of training."

We stood there watching Luke play with the puppies. I silently prayed one more time.

"Honey, I think she's our dog. What do you think?"

He smiled at me, "Sure, let's take her."

The attendant opened the cage, but she wouldn't come out. John tried calling her, but still she didn't move. The man interrupted,

"Ahh, I'd better get her." He picked her up and carried her back to the office.

While the keeper worked on the papers, John went to the truck to get a rope. When he came back he slipped the rope around her neck and started to walk, but she resisted.

"Oh, she doesn't know how to lead. No one has taught her," the attendant announced.

John tried pulling on the rope, but the dog just pulled back. John looked at the gentleman and then he looked at me.

"Great! Just great!" he leaned over and picked her up and started carrying her out to the truck.

As I walked beside him he proclaimed, "So this is the dog, huh! She can't even walk on her own!"

John spent the next few weeks training her. After each session he came in excited,

"You know, she really is a smart dog. She catches on fast."

She caught on fast alright. It only took her a few weeks to figure out that the training was coming out of a book John was reading. When he left it hanging on the clothesline she spied it. I watched as she looked high above her head. Then all of a sudden she jumped up, grabbed it and started tearing it to shreds!!

Despite a rough beginning, she proved to be a grand dog—exactly what I prayed for. She watched after us and we grew to love her. I believe she loved us too.

In Reflection

After God answered our prayer about our dog, I came to realize that there is no detail of our lives that God is not concerned about. The older I get the more convinced I become that it is the little things, the ordinary things that make up a life that deserve our attention and our continual prayer.

The Challenge

Remembering to pray and not go ahead of the Spirit is a discipline that takes time to develop. Do you take matters into your own hands? Do you make quick decisions without checking with the Lord first?

The results could turn out alright, after all "a dog is a dog." However, you may be settling for "good enough" rather than the best. The "obvious choice" is not always the one the Lord would choose for you.

Think about your life today. What decisions are you struggling to make? When do you plan to ask the Lord for his wisdom? How about right now?

∞ **Further Study** ∞

"...and you shall anoint for Me the one whom I designate to you...Arise, anoint him; for this is he."

1 Samuel 16:3-12

"And everything you ask in prayer, believing, you shall receive."

Matthew 12:10

"With all prayer and petition pray at all times in the Spirit, with this in view, be on the alert with all perseverance and petition for all the saints..."

Ephesians 6:18

"Don't fret or worry. Instead of worrying, pray."

Philippians 4:6

1, 2, 3 – Go

Nathan, two and half, knew how to "cut the corner" from the ladder to the swimming pool's edge. His face showed his pride of accomplishment.

"Oh, Nathan, you're just a regular fish," his instructor encouraged. "I'm so proud of you. Today, you're ready to try something different. I want you to come away from the edge of the pool with me. We're going to swim in the middle, down to the deep end where the diving board is. You're going to climb out. Jump off the diving board, right into my hands."

I caught the look on my son's face. He gasped in disbelief, then turned from her and hung onto the side of the pool yelling:

"No, I'm not! No, I'm not! And you can't make me!"

He kept protesting loudly, as she peeled him off the side of the pool and carried him over to the middle.

1, 2, 3 – Go

"Nathan, I will be with you all the way down to the end. You only have to do this one time and then you'll be all done."

I'm not sure Nathan heard the reassurance she gave him, because he was screaming the whole time. She pushed him out, away from her body, and then calmly counted:

"1, 2, 3," and let him go.

He swam towards her. When she bobbed him up for air, he came up shrieking,

"I'm not going to do this!"

She let him go again and there was silence as he once again made his way toward her. She again bobbed him up for air and again he squealed,

"No!"

I was embarrassed as all the other parents watched my child. I can't quite say how his instructor got him out of the pool and onto the diving board, but she did. He jumped to her, finishing his lesson. He got out and ran to tell his friend. I rushed over to the edge of the pool to ask her:

"Why did he protest so violently? He had been content swimming back and forth from the pool's edge to the ladder. He knew he could do that, then why was he so mad?"

"Pressure."

"Pressure?" I echoed.

Where is the Water?

"Yes, pressure of the added responsibility. You see, when he is swimming back and forth from the ladder to the pool's edge, he is in his own secure little world."

"He feels comfortable with that, but when I take him out into the middle of the pool, and make him breathe while swimming in the water, even though I am right there to help him, he's yelling,

'I don't want this extra responsibility. I want to stay in my secure little world and not learn anything new, because learning something new demands too much of me. I don't want the responsibility. I feel pressured and I don't like it!'"

As she finished talking to me, I was stunned. She had touched a nerve. I too was screaming and kicking within me,

I can't handle this. I don't want the obligation of an unfinished log cabin, a business and debt.

It some how seemed safer to stay in my own little world and not learn anything new. I forgot that God said he would be with me, that he would teach me, like Nathan's instructor, how to "breathe" in his water, the water of the Holy Spirit.

In Reflection

Nathan's swimming instructor demonstrated to me how I needed to learn to breathe in the pressure places of my life; otherwise, I would wear myself out and sink under the weight of the demands of everyday life: husband, children, business and home management, civic and social pressures.

God was calling me to come out into the deep water with him, to trust him. He would not only teach me how to swim—how to live in hard situations, but to jump off the diving board and thrive! But I was too afraid. What if he asked me to do something way beyond my capability and comfort zone?

I was having trouble letting go of the edge— letting go of what I already knew. Even if I was a pressure cooker that given enough heat, enough stress, would explode in anger. God was inviting me to cooperate with him. He would instruct me on how to take responsibility for my life. But first I needed to humble myself, to ask, to trust that he would show me where to start.

Like the swimming teacher, he promised to be with me, in the deep water, all the way to the end.

The Challenge

In what areas are you struggling to stay afloat in your life? Have you heard God calling you to come out of your comfort zone? What stops you from trusting him?

Have you already prayed for his help, but he seems not to have answered? Wait. Spend time listening. Learn how to discern the answers of God coming from an unexpected place—your everyday life. He walks with you. Ask for his help to open your eyes. Ask him to open your ears so you might hear his voice.

∞ Further Study ∞

"Go and tell this people: 'Be ever hearing, but never understanding; be ever seeing, but never perceiving."

Isaiah 6:9-10

"Pay attention! Are you deaf? Open your eyes! Are you blind? You're my servant, and you're not looking! You're my messenger, and you're not listening! The very people I depend upon, servants of God, blind as a bat—willfully blind! You've seen a lot, but looked at nothing. You've heard everything, but listened to nothing."

Isaiah 42:18-25

1, 2, 3 – Go

"'Whoever believes in me, as the Scripture has said, steams of living water will flow from within him.' By this he meant the Spirit, whom those who believed in him were later to receive."

John 7:38-39

"What matters most to me is to finish what God started: the job the Master Jesus gave me of letting everyone I meet know all about this incredibly extravagant generosity of God."

Acts 20:24

If He Was Your Son, What Would You Do?

The echo of teenage laughter and the smell of chlorine hit me as we walked through the front door of the aquatic center. I could feel the excitement, as the State Championships were about to start. We took three steps in when our son's coach greeted us.

"I don't want you to panic when you see Nathan," her eyes were filled with concern. "He seems to be alright."

Overcoming the urge to push past her and rush into the pool area I asked her:

"What happened?"

"We are not sure. He has this gigantic lip that keeps swelling."

Lip? I was thinking to myself, *is that all?* I was relieved.

As we walked towards the pool, I spotted Nathan. He was making the most out of his big lip by pretending to be a monster. His teammates were laughing as he snarled in a deep voice:

"Hey, my name is Mongo!"

If He Was Your Son What Would You Do?

As soon as he saw us he ran over.

"Hey, Mom, Dad..."

Before we could respond he was off and running again. I'd never seen a lip that huge. It reminded me of a small Caribbean banana!

My husband and I found a place to sit on the bleachers. After we watched Nathan swim one of his individual events a woman behind us tapped me on the shoulder.

"Is that your son?" She pointed at Nathan in the team holding area. He and his teammates were laughing as he used his lip as a humorous intimidation tactic.

"Yes."

"I'm an RN."

I must have given her a confused look because she added, "A registered nurse. Your son is in anaphylactic shock."

She might as well have been speaking a foreign language. I looked at her like:

What are you talking about?

"His lip—it's part of his breathing apparatus. You cannot let him get back into the water. He could drown."

She had my attention. I turned to look at her directly. She continued,

"You need to take him to the nearest hospital. Go now. Don't wait until after the meet."

Where is the Water?

I was familiar with that word "now." I went into immediate action. I jumped up from the bleachers and turned to look at John. He didn't hesitate.

"I'll find out where the nearest hospital is," he said as he headed toward the coach.

I walked to the team holding area and yelled,

"Nathan!" He must have recognized the tone in my voice, because he ran over to me right away. His face gave the expression of,

What's wrong?

I explained what the RN told me and that Dad was informing the coach we were headed for the hospital. It didn't take him long to throw on his sweats.

When we walked through the door of the emergency room the nurse took one look at our son and said,

"Follow me."

John dealt with the paperwork while I followed Nathan and the nurse.

The doctor had him lay down. As he explained to both of us what was happening he gave Nathan a shot. John arrived just in time for the doctor's questions:

"What did you take?" the doctor asked Nathan.

Nathan looked confused.

"You are allergic to something. What did you take?"

Nathan thought for a minute, "I had a sore

throat. It started on Thursday night. It started getting worse. I didn't have any Tylenol. One of the kids had Ibuprofen, so I took it."

"How many did you take?"

"I've taken two every four hours since last night."

"When did your lip start swelling?"

"I don't know. Some time last night. When I woke up this morning it was pretty big."

"You've had an allergic reaction to the medicine. But the shot I gave you will settle it down. You won't be swimming today."

I caught the look on Nathan's face. My heart sank with his. I attempted to persuade the doctor:

"But it's State Championships."

"I know, but..." he started to answer.

"It's his senior year. He won't have another chance."

The doctor looked at Nathan. He looked at each one of us. He attempted once again to explain how the medicine would work in Nathan's body.

"I have given him Benadryl to arrest the swelling and adrenaline to increase the rate of speed of the Benadryl through his body. He won't be swimming."

Nathan wanted the doctor to understand:

"But I feel fine. I'm alright." He didn't want to let his team down.

Where is the Water?

The doctor was sympathetic. He understood Nathan's desire.

"It's a tough break," he told Nathan as he tapped him on the knee.

I said to the doctor, "If he was your son, what would you do?"

The doctor looked down, thought for a moment, shook his head "no", then broke out into a big grin and looked at me, "I'd let him swim."

The atmosphere in the room changed immediately. We were all grinning and excited. Then the doctor turned to Nathan and said:

"I want you to understand, Son. You won't be breaking any records. In fact, if you were swimming in the Olympics the shot of adrenaline I just gave you would disqualify you. They wouldn't let you swim, but this is State. They do not have those rules."

Nathan was visibly pleased as he intently listened to the doctor's instructions:

"I want you to promise me that if you feel tired, if you feel like you're having any trouble breathing at all, that you will get out of the water. There is no shame in saying, 'I can't do this.' Do you understand?"

Nathan was nodding his head "yes."

"You'll be lucky to make your time. The Benadryl I gave you is going to slow you down—a lot."

Nathan assured him, "I understand."

If He Was Your Son What Would You Do?

Once in the parking lot of the aquatic center the three of us bowed our heads and prayed.

"Lord, watch over Nathan as he swims today. Help his team do their best, help Nathan to swim his best." I had to add, "Help him listen to you Lord, if he needs to get out."

When we walked back into the aquatic center the coach let us know Nathan had not missed his last events. They agreed he would let the alternate swim the relay and he would swim his individual event. He made his personal time. Nathan, the team and the coach overcame a huge obstacle and persevered.

In Reflection

A professional photographer took Nathan's picture as he swam his last lap. You can't see his big lip. You can't even say for sure that it is Nathan in the photograph. But I know it's him. I keep it in my office to remind me what perseverance looks like.

This was the two and half year old who did not want to come away from the pool's edge, who did not want to learn to breathe while swimming in the water.

Many years later he had made it to State Championships, but there was a glitch. There was going to be a challenge. There was no shame in saying, "I can't do this." But he wasn't going to give up without at least trying.

We prayed and Nathan believed the Lord would help him swim. The doc said he would not be able to make his personal time. On his own maybe not, but with God's help *"all things are possible."*

I love inspiring stories of perseverance and determination. At the end of the year Nathan's team voted him Most Inspirational.

The Challenge

Fear can stop you from reaching your dreams. You may even have experts telling you,

"It's impossible."

But how do you know what you can do, until you've tried? There is no shame in trying. If it doesn't work out you can be sure the "experts" will be the first to let you know.

But if you listen to those who have never tried you may miss your big dream. Call on the Holy Spirit—the inner wisdom and strength that helps you overcome your obstacles. Believe the Lord has a purpose, a dream for you. When you are willing to ask him he gives you the courage to capture your dream.

If He Was Your Son What Would You Do?

What dream will you pursue with the Holy Spirit? Write it down. Pick a verse from Scripture that will help you remember. Post it on a 3x5 card. When you are tempted to forget read the verse out loud then pray.

∞ Further Study ∞

"Jesus looked hard at them and said, 'No chance at all if you think you can pull it off yourself. Every chance in the world if you trust God to do it.'"

Mathew 19:26

"By your perseverance you will win your souls."

Luke 21:19

"And we know that God causes all things to work for good to those who love God, to those who are called according to His purpose."

Romans 8:28

"Anyone who meets a testing challenge head-on and manages to stick it out is mighty fortunate. For such persons loyally in love with God, the reward is life and more life."

James 1:12

Are You Alright?

Walking along the single lane university campus road, I was praying,

"Lord, please don't let anything happen to John or me. Please watch over us."

I had just become engaged. I wanted the Lord's protection for us.

I turned right onto another single lane campus road and headed up the hill toward the student commons. I watched a man on my right get out of a large delivery truck that was parked at an angle in front of the men's gym.

He used the tailgate of the truck, which doubled as an elevator, to lower the dolly full of books to the ground. Before he turned to go into the gym, he raised the elevator so it was even with the bed of the truck.

As I watched him walk toward the building, I heard a voice within me say:

"What would you do if that delivery truck started to roll down the hill?"

Are You Alright?

"I'd run up the hill as fast as I could."

"No! You'll be crushed between the tree and the truck."

"What tree?"

"That tree."

My eyes seemed to be directed toward a large tree on the left side of the campus road.

"Run behind the tree. Go NOW!"

Immediately, the truck began to roll!! It was rolling backwards at an angle down the hill towards me!

I ran to the left for the far side of the tree as instructed. SMASH! The splitting of bark and crunching metal filled my ears. Standing on the other side of the noise—was me! My knees went weak. My brain flooded with realization.

"You'll be crushed between the tree and the truck."

Slowly I moved from behind the tree and the DMV trailer parked next to it. I began playing the whole scene again in my mind. As I tried to grasp what just happened, a student came down the hill from campus:

"Are you alright? Oh, wow! Come over here. Sit down on the curb. You don't look too good. Are you okay? That truck just about hit you. Here, sit here."

Just then the delivery man came running out of the building,

"I'm sorry! I'm sorry! I forgot to turn on the emergency brake!"

Where is the Water?

The guy who had instructed me to sit down stood up and started yelling his disdain for the truck driver. Then he sat down and kept asking me if I was okay.

I was speechless. All I could do was nod my head, "Yes."

As I sat on the curb, I realized someone had told me what to do before that truck starting rolling at an angle down the hill. If I had not been listening…if I had not been praying…I was dumbfounded.

"*How can I explain to this guy what just happened? I can't. What can I say? 'A voice, somewhere inside of me told me what to do; told me where and when to run.'*"

I had never heard that voice before. I knew it was the Lord. He had immediately answered my prayer. He protected me.

In Reflection

Often I wonder what would have happened if I had not already been in prayer. Would I have heard? Would I have obeyed? Would I have run and been crushed between the truck and the tree as the voice said?

It was an ordinary day as I walked toward campus; nothing special about it, until I prayed and the extraordinary changed my life.

Are You Alright?

The Challenge

Belief that God truly watches over and protects you is pretty convincing when dramatic things happen to you and you are okay. Do you believe he's watching and protecting you even when things do not turn out as you planned?

Where in your everyday life do you need to ask God to help you clearly see and hear him?

Remember ordinary days turn into extraordinary days when you become aware of God reaching out to you.

∞ Further Study ∞

"He who dwells in the shelter of the Most High will abide in the shadow of the Almighty."

Psalm 91:1

"...all things for which you pray and ask, Believe that you have received them, and they shall be granted."

Mark 11:24

"...after He had finished [praying], one of His disciples said to Him, Lord, teach us to pray..."

Luke 11:1-13

Do As I Tell You

"Lord, help Mom to find her hairbrush so she won't look so tacky."

Luke, at ten years old, laughed at his own cleverness; then he left the living room to go outside.

I headed toward the kitchen and started washing the dishes. When I had almost finished I heard the Lord say:

"Make your bed and you will find your hairbrush."

I was so excited, *"Thanks Lord!"*

I rushed to my bedroom and pushed the comforter onto the floor. I looked all around the bottom of the bed and then the floor. I looked through the rest of the bed covers, but there was no hairbrush. I sat down on the side of the bed:

"Lord, there is no hairbrush here."

"I said, 'Make your bed and you will find your hairbrush.'"

"Hmm."

I began to make my bed, all the while looking for my brush. But it did not magically appear. As I was bent over smoothing out the bedspread, my eyes very carefully followed my hand. It pointed to my makeup vanity across the room. There, peeking out of the skirt of my vanity was my hairbrush. It had been knocked on the floor and kicked slightly under the vanity.

"I found it! Thanks Lord."

"The lesson is not about finding your hairbrush. The lesson is obedience."

"What?"

"Do what I say, not what you think I said, or thought I meant, but what I said. I said, 'Make your bed and you will find your hairbrush.' What did you do?"

"I tore my bed apart looking for my brush."

"Yes, the exact opposite of what I told you. Do as I tell you."

In Reflection

In my excitement I interpreted what I thought the Lord had meant. I was wrong. When I did exactly as I was told, that is when the answer to my prayer came.

I do not always understand how my obedience will make a difference in the requests I have made to the Lord. It took many lessons to understand not to go ahead of the

Spirit, not to go ahead of the leadings of the Lord.

I am still learning I need to do exactly as he says, not take my own steps, but wait for the steps he gives—one at a time. Second guessing only makes a mess of things; a mess much bigger than an unmade bed.

The Challenge

Do you like to be in control of the events of your life? Do you sometimes say, "I'll do it myself, I do it better"?

Only God has the foresight to see what lies ahead. It takes making a few of your own mistakes to realize you can trust him. Risk humility and ask him for his help. Be sure and ask him for the courage to follow his wisdom. Then stay alert to his leading.

God's timing is different than yours. Be patient. Wait. Believe he will answer.

In the meantime what can you do to prepare yourself? Is there something you already know you need to do, but you have been procrastinating?

Remember to wait for God's instruction then take the initiative to take care of that one thing in which you have been delaying. It may be the first step God has been waiting for you to take.

Believe God has a much bigger plan than you can imagine. Ask yourself, *What has God been asking me to do to prepare myself to follow his plan one step at a time?*

∞ Further Study ∞

"But the loving-kindness of the LORD is from everlasting to everlasting on those who fear him, And His righteousness to children's children, to those who keep His covenant, and who remember His precepts to do them."

Psalm 103:17-18

"'I know the plans that I have for you,' declares the LORD, 'plans for welfare and not for calamity to give you a future and a hope. Then you will call upon Me and come and pray to Me, and I will listen to you. And you will seek Me and find Me, when you search for Me with all your heart.'"

Jeremiah 29:11-13

"For to this end also I wrote that I might put you to the test, whether you are obedient in all things."

2 Corinthians 2:9

Do You Really Want to Know?

Driving from our rural home toward a nearby town, I concentrated on praying. The two lane highway was crowded with cars and trucks. The road was nicknamed "Bloody Alley"—not without reason. Its narrow shoulders are unforgiving if your wheel should drop off the edge.

There was a three quarter ton old Ford pickup in front of me. I prayed:

"Should I pass it?"

"How fast is it going?" came the voice within me.

I looked down at my mileage gauge, *"55."*

"Hmm...sounds like the speed limit."

True, I would have to exceed the speed limit to pass. I decided to be content just following.

A few minutes later, a long line of cars were in the oncoming lane coming from the nearby town. The voice within me said,

"Do you see that little blue car?"

I was not paying attention. I looked down the road. About eight car lengths ahead in the lane of oncoming traffic was a little blue car peeking in and out of his lane. He went back in—then he peeked out again:

Do You Really Want to Know?

"What is he doing?"
"He's going to pass."
"Pass! How is he going to do that?"

There was a line of traffic on his side of the road and I guessed there was a long line behind me.

"There is going to be a head-on collision."

"What?!" I touched my brakes slightly and turned the wheel of my car to the left. I saw a small car crowed with people and then a white van packed with farm workers.

"Lord, I don't want to hit them. What do I do?"

The wheel turned slightly back to the right as I glanced out my window to the left. The driver of a log truck was looking at me like I was crazy. Immediately, I heard inside of me,

"Hit your brakes, NOW!"

My foot was already on the brake. I slammed it down harder as I heard the screeching of tires from what I guessed to be a massive vehicle behind me.

I watched as the driver of the Ford in front of me hit her brakes and skid to the right. The tailgate of her pickup bounced in the air as she hit head long into the little blue car.

I expected the screeching sound of tires behind me to end with a bang, but it never happened. My car came to a silent halt. I got out of the car and exchanged glances with the log truck driver, who with his look said,

You are one lucky lady.

Proceeding to walk around my car, I found I could have passed untouched between the log truck and the Ford pickup.

I discovered the large vehicle behind me was a dump truck. The driver rushed over to me:

"I thought you were a goner for sure! When you hit your brakes, I thought the Toyota [the blue car] was making a left hand turn. I started slowing down. When I began to see what was happening, I was going to head for the ditch. But when I saw you turned your wheel to the left, I changed my mind. Then I started yelling,

'Don't you see the log truck?! Don't you see the log truck?!'"

"They advise us with these big trucks to 'just keep it straight, brake and hope for the best. By the time everyone gets stopped no one is where you expect them to be.' If I hadn't of already been brakin' I'd of killed you all for sure."

Do You Really Want to Know?

In Reflection

"Pray without ceasing" took on a new meaning after that day. I also saw obedience in a new light. I realized if I had passed the Ford pickup and not listened and obeyed, I would have been the lead car in the accident.

Continual prayer kept me from being plowed over by the log truck in the other lane and the dump truck behind me.

I tried to tell the insurance investigator I was a morning person, so I had quick reflexes, but she wasn't buying it.

"Why did you brake before the Ford pickup? From the marks on the road the police could tell you braked before she did. What would make you do that?"

What indeed, I thought to myself. Then I said,

"Do you really want to know?"

The Challenge

Believing the Lord watches over you and takes care of you may challenge your faith. Believe it. Come to expect it, hope in it. Learn to STOP, LOOK and LISTEN for his voice. Doubt will tempt you to brush away his promptings. Believing will save more than your physical life.

Where is the Water?

Ask yourself:

Do I pray to the Lord while going about my daily activities or am I unconscious of his presence?

Do I keep "every thought captive to the obedience of Christ" or do I pray only when I need something from him?

Am I alert and listening for God's wisdom or do I tune him out?

Do I really want to know what God has to say to me or am I afraid that if I hear him he might ask me to do something that I don't want to do?

There is a reward for staying alert to God's voice. His wisdom is ever ready to protect you from harm.

∞ Further Study ∞

"Keep me as the apple of the eye; Hide me in the shadow of Thy wings."

Psalm 17:8

"Blessed is the man, blessed the woman, who listens to me, awake and ready for me each morning, alert and responsive as I start my day's work. When you find me, you find life, real life, to say nothing of God's good pleasure."

Proverbs 8:35

"For wisdom is protection just as money is protection.

Do You Really Want to Know?

But the advantage of knowledge is that wisdom preserves the lives of its possessors."

Ecclesiastes 7:12

"We demolish arguments and every pretension that sets itself up against the knowledge of God, and we are taking every thought captive to the obedience of Christ."

2 Corinthians 10:5

"Always be joyful. Keep on praying. No matter what happens, always be thankful, for this is God's will for you who belong to Christ Jesus."

1 Thessalonians 5:16-17

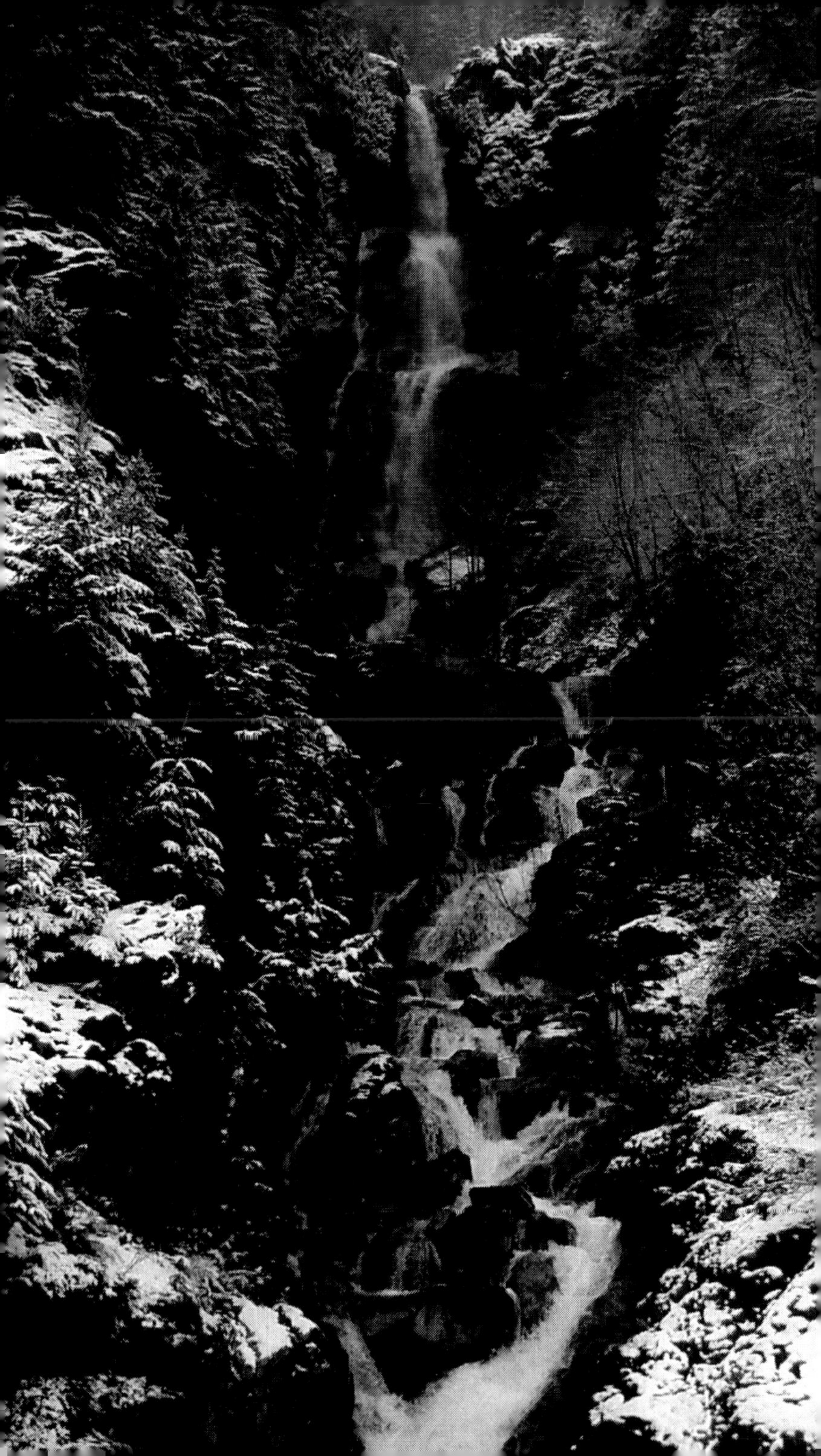

Okay, You Lead and I Will Follow

Decorating our guest room on a slim budget was going to be a challenge. John already had the paint and my Dad had built the bed. Other than that we were starting from scratch. I prayed the Lord would help me stretch our dollars.

The first thing we needed was a bedspread. I took my Victorian soap container with me to the mall to match the rose pattern and color scheme. The sales lady showed me a bedspread set that matched perfectly and it was on sale. However, it was $50 over my budget.

After closer inspection, I decided to take the set to the sales clerk behind the counter.

"It looks like it has been opened."

She pulled the set out of the zippered container, "It's missing the bottom skirt. Let me see what I can do."

She checked with the sales manager, but a $25 discount still wasn't enough.

"Well," I told her, "you can hold it for me, until I look around the mall some more."

Okay, You Lead and I Will Follow

As I walked away I heard the Lord say,

"Wait. Just wait. You need sheets. Go over and look at the sheets." So I did.

The original sales lady who had helped me pick out the bedspread set came over to help:

"Did you get the bedspread?"

"No. The ruffle is missing, but the sales manager will only give me a $25 discount. Like I told you, I only have $100 to spend on it."

"Do you want it for $100?"

"Yes, but..."

"Come on then," she motioned for me to follow her. I grabbed up the white sheets I had picked out and followed, "I'll sell it to you for $100."

"Can you do that?" I asked in disbelief.

"Of course I can!" she answered confidently.

I paid for my purchases and headed for the car. I stopped at a resale shop on the way home. I wasn't looking for anything in particular. I just liked to check periodically. I was on my way out the door when I heard:

"Do you see that picture over there?" It was the Lord getting my attention.

I asked, *"What picture?"*

"You have been looking at a couch. Look above it. Do you see the picture?"

Where is the Water?

My eyes were drawn up. There was a Victorian picture that looked like it would match my bedspread. I retrieved a pillow sham from the car and laid it on the couch.

"Wow! We just got that picture in today," the comment came from behind me. The sales lady continued:

"I have been looking for a picture for my room for a year. That looks like a perfect match for you."

"You think so?" I needed a second opinion.

"The frame is actually gold roses. That matches the roses on your bedspread."

She was right. It was perfect. I decided to buy it. I stopped at one more place on my way home, but the decorative trees I looked at were too expensive.

Venturing out the next day to look for bathmats for the guest bathroom, I checked out Goodwill, but they had nothing to offer so I went next door. Finding what I needed I returned to the car and as I was putting my purchases in the trunk I heard:

"*You were going to get your mother a basket for Easter.*"

"*Oh, that's right, thanks!*" I walked back into Goodwill to see what I could find.

"*Do you see that tree over there?*" I heard within me.

"What tree?" I said out loud. Then I quickly looked around to see if anyone had noticed me talking to myself!!

"That tree right in front of you."

I looked down the walkway to the other end of the store. There was a tall decorative tree just like the one I had been eyeing the other day at another store. I thought to myself,

Was that tree there when I came in to look for bathmats? It's right next to the bathmats. How did I miss it?

I checked the price. Wow! It was less than a quarter of the price of the tree I had seen yesterday at the other store. I decided to get it.

The guest room was shaping up, but I was not done yet.

The next day I was coming back from visiting a friend when I heard the Lord say:

"Turn here."

"Turn where? There is nothing here. This is just a wide spot in the road."

But I turned right and there to the left was a thrift store. When I went in I didn't know what I was looking for, so I listened intently:

"Do you see it?" the Lord asked.

"See what? What am I looking for?"

"Over there, behind the desk—the picture."

Where is the Water?

Almost hidden in the corner on the floor was a gold-framed picture in the same coloring as the one I had bought the day before. I looked closer. Yep, the frame was made of gold roses. I also spotted a freestanding lamp that would work in my Victorian room.

Later in the week the Lord directed me to a gold-framed mirror for the guest room at a second hand shop. Then I sat down and said:

"Okay, I know this is not about putting my guest room together. It's done. I appreciate all your help, but what is this all about?" I waited for an answer.

"If you let me, I'll show you how to put a ministry together just like I did your guest bedroom. Follow my lead and I will show you what to do."

I was stunned. He was right. I did not know how to do what he asked. What did I know about writing a book, starting a ministry, putting up a website, and forming a team?

"Okay, *you lead and I will follow,"* I answered.

In Reflection

I just wanted a guest room. The Lord had something bigger in mind. He used my willingness to be obedient in the little things to teach me how to be obedient in the big things. Because of his grace, he put together a beautiful Victorian guest bedroom that matched my budget.

He helped me finish three books. He showed me how to do the work. He sent volunteers with the expertise to do each piece of the project exactly when I needed them. He encouraged me to focus on the task at hand, listen to his voice and do exactly what he said. If I tried to jump ahead he gently reminded me that he was leading and I needed to follow. He assured me he already had the plan and he would show me one step at a time.

He is not done yet! His grace and guidance goes far beyond guest bedrooms, books and team building. I can't wait to see where he is taking us next!

The Challenge

You may have your own ideas of what you need to do and where you need to go to accomplish your goals. Unless you are open to wait for the Lord's help you may miss the big picture—the end design.

Where is the Water?

Impatience leads down a path that not only has a dead end, but you will need to turn around and start over. Learn to discipline yourself in the little things. When you are ready, God will give you bigger things to manage.

In what aspect of your life do you need to let God lead? Are you willing to follow his lead?

When you know the answer to those questions don't delay, instead take the initiative to move forward. Remember you are not going alone.

God can accomplish what he asks you to do. Trust him. Get ready for a new adventure.

∞ Further Study ∞

"But you, be strong and do not lose courage, for there is reward for your work."

2 Chronicles 15:7

"Wait for the LORD; Be strong, and let your heart take courage; Yes, wait for the Lord."

Psalm 27:14

"And He said to them, 'Follow Me, and I will make you fishers of men.' And they immediately left their nets, and followed Him."

Matthew 4:19-20

Okay, You Lead and I Will Follow

"He said, 'Good servant! Great work! because you've been trustworthy in this small job, I'm making you governor of the town.'"

Luke 19:17

"He said, 'That's what I mean: Risk your life and get more than you ever dreamed of. Play it safe and end up holding the bag.'"

Luke 19:26

"My sheep recognize my voice; I know them, and they follow me. I give them eternal life, and they will never perish. No one will snatch them away from me, for my Father has given them to me, and he is more powerful than anyone else."

John 10:27-29

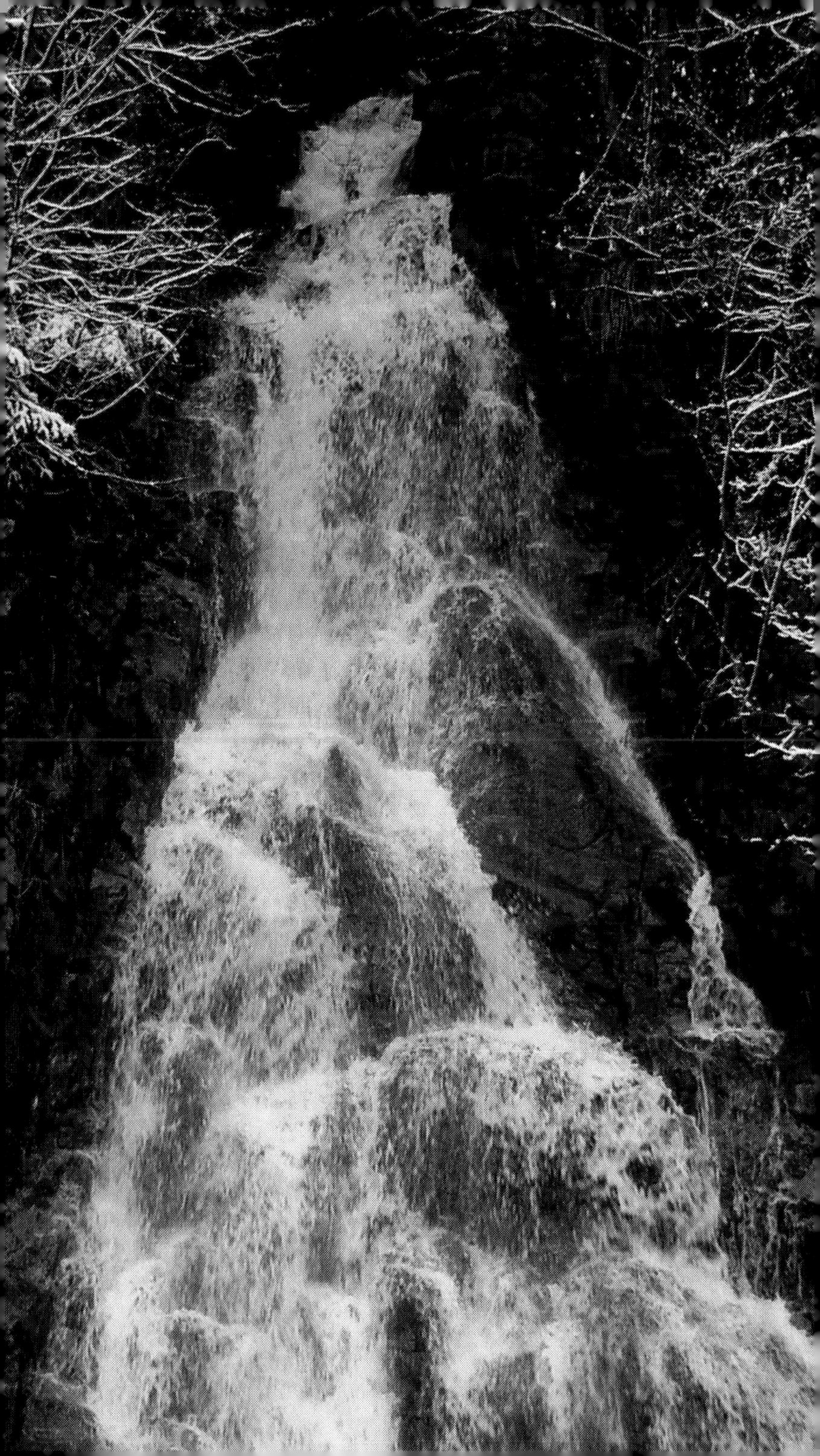

I Thought You Were an Angel

Early in the morning I opened the wood stove and threw a chunk of wood on the hot coals before settling into my prayer chair. No one was up yet and I wanted to keep it that way. I grabbed my Bible; read, prayed and then sat in silence.

In my mind a woman's face appeared. The Lord said:

"I want you to take a blank card and on the left side write: 'Seek ye first the kingdom of God, and his righteousness; and all these things shall be added unto you.' On the right side write: 'I love you' then sign it, 'Jesus.' Give it to the woman."

"But, Lord," I argued, *"I don't even know this woman. Where would I find her?"*

"Go to the Market."

I obeyed out of curiosity. I wanted to see if I actually saw her face.

When I arrived at the Market, sure enough, there she was. She was a checker; when I had shopped there before I had not consciously noticed her.

I Thought You Were An Angel

I put Nathan, my two and half year old, into the seat of the cart, checked my list and started looking for vegetables. As I cruised through the store I asked the Lord,

"How am I going to do this without making a scene?"

I didn't want to be embarrassed or cause confusion. I had no clear picture in my mind of what I was supposed to do. The checker left her stand and started rearranging some of the fruit.

"Now, Lord? Do I give it to her now?" I silently inquired.

"When she hands you the sales receipt hand her the card," he answered.

It seemed simple enough. When I finished shopping I made my way to the checkout stand, but she was gone.

Oh, well, I thought to myself, *maybe another day.*

I stood, third person back at another checkout line.

"I can help you over here."

The female voice was coming from the left. At first I thought I would pretend I didn't hear her, but she repeated a little louder,

"I can help you over here."

I smiled and wheeled my cart to her checkout. She seemed friendly and we made small talk. As she handed me the receipt I took it and then quickly handed her the card.

"What's this?" she inquired.

"A card," I answered.

"Who's it from?"

I smiled and said to the Lord, *"You did not tell me she was going to ask all these questions."*

She tilted her head like a kitten who is watching something curious. She started to open it! Quickly I blurted out,

"It's from a friend. Ah, you can open it later—on your break."

I smiled as she agreed and stuck it in her apron pocket.

Relieved, I left the store and went to my friend's house. As I reviewed my morning with my friend she said:

"I know who she is."

"What do you mean, 'You know who she is?'"

"I don't know her, but our church bus picks up her kids. She used to wear wedding rings, but she is not wearing them anymore."

Two weeks later another friend confirmed the wedding rings,

"Yes, she took off her rings for awhile, but now they're back. She seems friendlier—happier."

I Thought You Were An Angel

I avoided the Market for a least a couple of months. When I returned she must not have recognized me, because she said nothing. The rings were definitely on her hand.

A year and half later, we were getting ready to move out of the area. I just had to know the rest of the story before we left town. I went over to the Market. After I picked up a few vegetables I stood in her checkout line.

When it was my turn I watched as she punched in the numbers. Then I asked her:

"Do you remember me?"

She gave me her attention, as if she were looking at me for the first time.

"No. Do I know you?"

"Well, no. But about a year and half ago I gave you a card."

She stopped checking my purchases and listened.

"It said, 'Seek ye first the kingdom of God...'"

"That was you! I thought you were an angel or something. I still have that card. My husband and I were talking about separation. Things were not going well. I had been praying. Then you showed up. I thought you were an angel!"

She smiled at me. I smiled back as she continued:

"I showed it to my husband. The card said, 'Seek ye first the kingdom of God and his righteousness.'"

"We looked it up and read the whole passage. We were in rough times. We started praying together. We went back to church!"

"How are things now?"

She broke out into a big grin,

"Good. Real good."

I handed her the money for my purchases. She handed me the receipt. As I left I silently said,

"Thank you, Lord."

In Reflection

I often have no idea what is going on behind the scenes in someone's life when the Lord calls me to be his hands and feet. Many of the people God calls me to speak to are strangers to me. I don't always get to hear the rest of the story. But when I do, I don't argue as much the next time God calls me. In fact, I'm getting bolder!

The Challenge

Have you heard the quiet promptings of the Lord encouraging you to reach out to be his hands and feet? Do you shut his voice down declaring, "It's none of my business!"?

I Thought You Were An Angel

How can you encourage someone else? A kind word could lift another's day. A card, a single flower, a balloon, a meal, a bag of groceries or some small token of God's care can give them the light they need to get through a dark day.

It's not too late to tune in to God's voice rather than tune out. You may be the "angel" of grace the Lord has decided to call on today. Take a chance. Believe you are the answer to someone else's prayer. For sure you will change an ordinary day into an extraordinary day!

Ask him,

"Who do you want me to reach out to today?"

Stay alert! Believe he will answer your small prayer.

∞ Further Study ∞

"I sought the LORD, and he answered me; he delivered me from all my fears."

Psalm 34:41

"So do not fear, for I am with you;... for I am your God. I will strengthen you and help you; I will uphold you with my righteous right hand."

Isaiah 41:10

Where is the Water?

"If God gives such attention to the appearance of wildflowers—most of which are never even seen—don't you think he'll attend to you, take pride in you, do his best for you? What I'm trying to do here is to get you to relax, to not be so preoccupied with getting, so you can respond to God's giving. People who don't know God and the way he works fuss over these things, but you know both God and how he works. Steep your life in God-reality, God-initiative, God-provisions. Don't worry about missing out. You'll find all your everyday human concerns will be met."

Matthew 6:30-33

"Cast all your anxiety on him because he cares for you."

I Peter 5:7

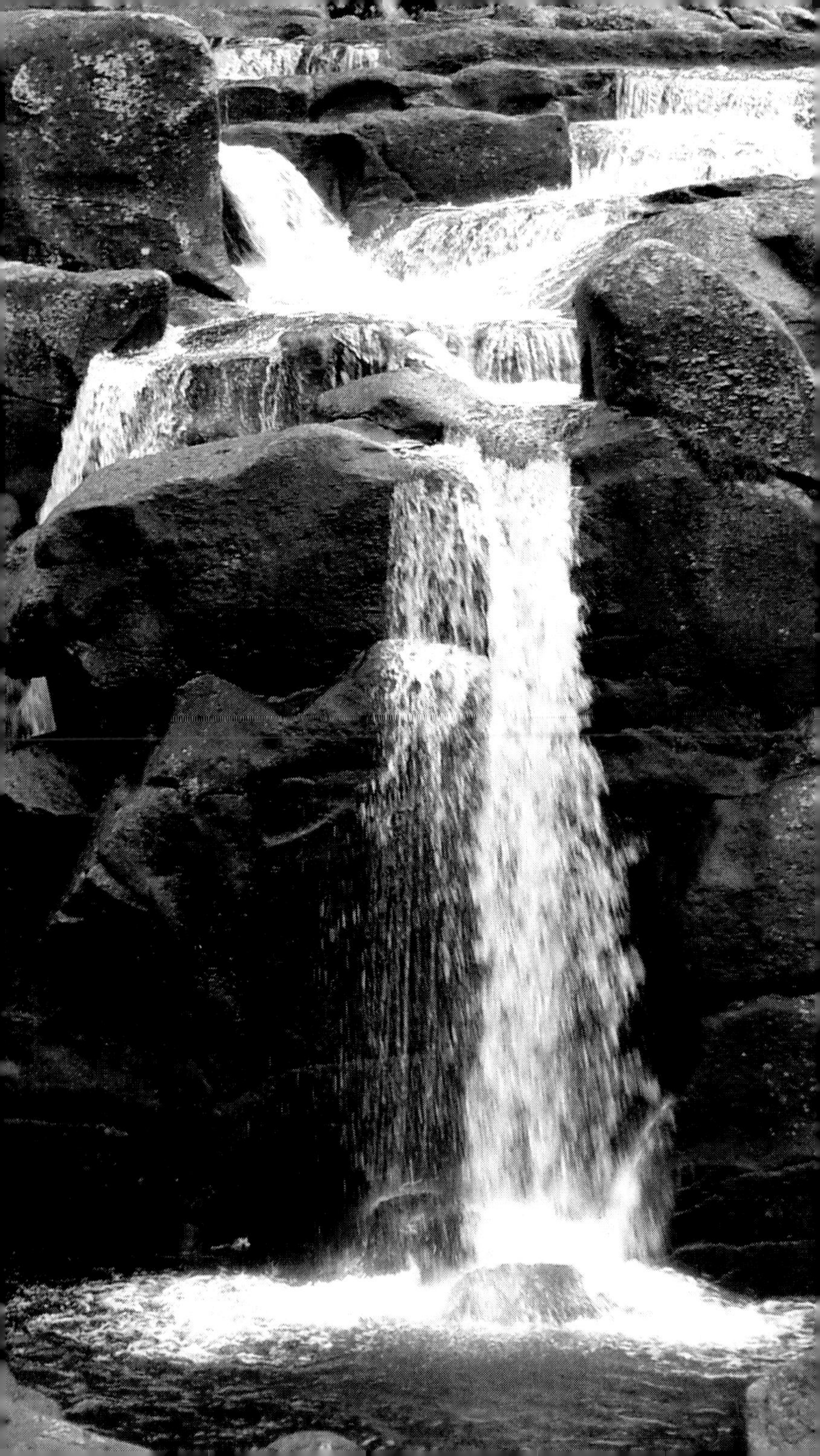

Tell Her She's Beautiful

Everywhere I went that Thursday I saw her. Tall, immaculately dressed, every hair in place, makeup just right on her flawless face. She was beautiful. She was one of those hard to miss kind of people that you see in the opening of a movie. Everyone else dressed in drab clothing, but she, the star, wore the bright fashion statement of the year.

The following Sunday I spotted her, she was three rows ahead of us sitting alone at church. During the morning greeting, I heard somewhere deep inside me say:

"Tell her she is as beautiful on the inside as she is on the outside."

"What?"

"Tell her she is as beautiful on the inside as she is on the outside."

I looked at my husband standing beside me. He was speaking to the people in front of us. In order to speak to her, I would need to squeeze past him and the two people sitting next to him, go three rows up, reach over four people and shake her hand.

People did not move from their seats during the morning welcoming. It was a foolish request. The moment to act had passed. The service continued.

The following Thursday when I went to town to run my errands, she haunted me. She seemed to be everywhere I went. She stood two people ahead of me in line at the local grocery store. An elderly man came from within the store and approached the checker,

"Would you please tell me where I might find the mustard?"

The checker responded by pointing over to the right of the store and quickly giving directions. As she went back to punching numbers on her machine, the old man looked confused.

The mysterious woman got out of line, greeted the elderly gentleman and directed him to follow her down an aisle on the other side of the store. When she returned she took her place at the end of the line.

Again on the next Sunday, she sat three pews in front of us, alone. Once more I heard,

"Tell her she is as beautiful on the inside as she is on the outside."

I knew the hound of heaven would give no peace until I obeyed. I crawled over my husband and the two

Where is the Water?

people sitting beside him. I heard him call after me,

"Where are you going?"

I pretended not to hear, as I made my way three rows up. The four people standing to greet one another, stopped to stare at me. She graciously took my hand as I blurted out,

"You're as beautiful on the inside as you are on the outside."

She looked stunned. I did not wait for a response. I turned and hurried to reclaim my seat three rows back.

As I crawled over the people sitting at the end of the pew, my husband, a bit perturbed asked:

"What are you doing? Why did you go clear up there? What..."

"Shhh...," I indicated the pastor was speaking. The time for chatting was over.

He glared a look of, *You will explain later.* I smiled and looked straight ahead in the direction of the pastor.

I saw her again two years later at the Christian bookstore. She was standing on a small platform surrounded by books. The shopkeeper was talking softly to her as the mysterious woman cried, listened and nodded her head.

Instantly the voice from within me said:

"Tell her she is as beautiful on the inside as she is on the outside."

Without hesitation this time, I approached her,

"You are as beautiful on the inside as you are on the outside."

The shopkeeper turned to scowl at me as if to say, *Can't you see we are busy here?*

As the attractive woman turned toward me, she stopped crying. Her eyes looked past me, as if she were seeing a scene somewhere behind me.

I asked her:

"Do you remember when I said that to you before?"

Catching her attention, she focused in on me.

"I could not tell you who said that to me. I remember the words though."

She looked past me again. The shopkeeper stepped back as the distraught woman described a moment out of the past:

"I was in church. I had been praying. I was telling the Lord he must think I am the most awful person, because I was getting ready to divorce my husband."

She glanced back at me, "He is taking me to court. He is trying to take my children away from me."

She again looked away from me staring at some drama the shopkeeper and I could not see. There was a long pause as none of us spoke.

Returning to look at me she said, "You give me hope."

I was confused. She explained,

"Those words at the time gave me hope. I knew the Lord had heard my prayer. I believe he is telling me once again, 'I'm taking care of it.'"

She turned around and hugged the shopkeeper. Her voice was filled with excitement. I turned and left the bookstore. Whatever I needed that day, it could wait.

Two weeks later as I was walking toward our town grocery store she was walking out,

"Oh, Diana," she beamed when she saw me. "I went to court. The judge gave my children to me."

"He made it so that my ex-husband can never again challenge me for them. Thank you! Thank you so much."

I was excited for her. As she walked away, rays of sunlight danced on her black hair. I never saw her again.

In Reflection

I may not know another's heart or how the message I am entrusted to bring to them will affect them. Obedience in the face of breaking social norms is not always easy, but I know from experience that the hound of heaven, the Holy Spirit will not let me ignore his voice. He could find someone else to deliver his message, but then I would miss out on the blessing of touching someone with his compassion.

The Challenge

What inner promptings from God have you been ignoring? The opportunity to grow waits on the other side of your obedience. Take a risk.

Stepping out in faith means you grow in boldness. Trust God wants to pour out his love to others through you. You may be the catalyst that brings hope to a dark situation.

Even if you do not know how your obedience affects another you will know the change in your own heart. There is no greater joy than knowing you are walking in God's love.

Who is God calling you to reach out to? When will you take a risk, leave your comfort zone and obey God?

∞ Further Study ∞

"I, even I, am he who blots out your transgressions, for my own sake, and remembers your sins no more."

Isaiah 43:25

"Because of the LORD's great love we are not consumed, for his compassions never fails."

Lamentations 3:22

"Therefore, there is now no condemnation for those who are in Christ Jesus, because through Christ Jesus the law of the Spirit of life set me free from the law of sin and death."

Romans 8:1-2

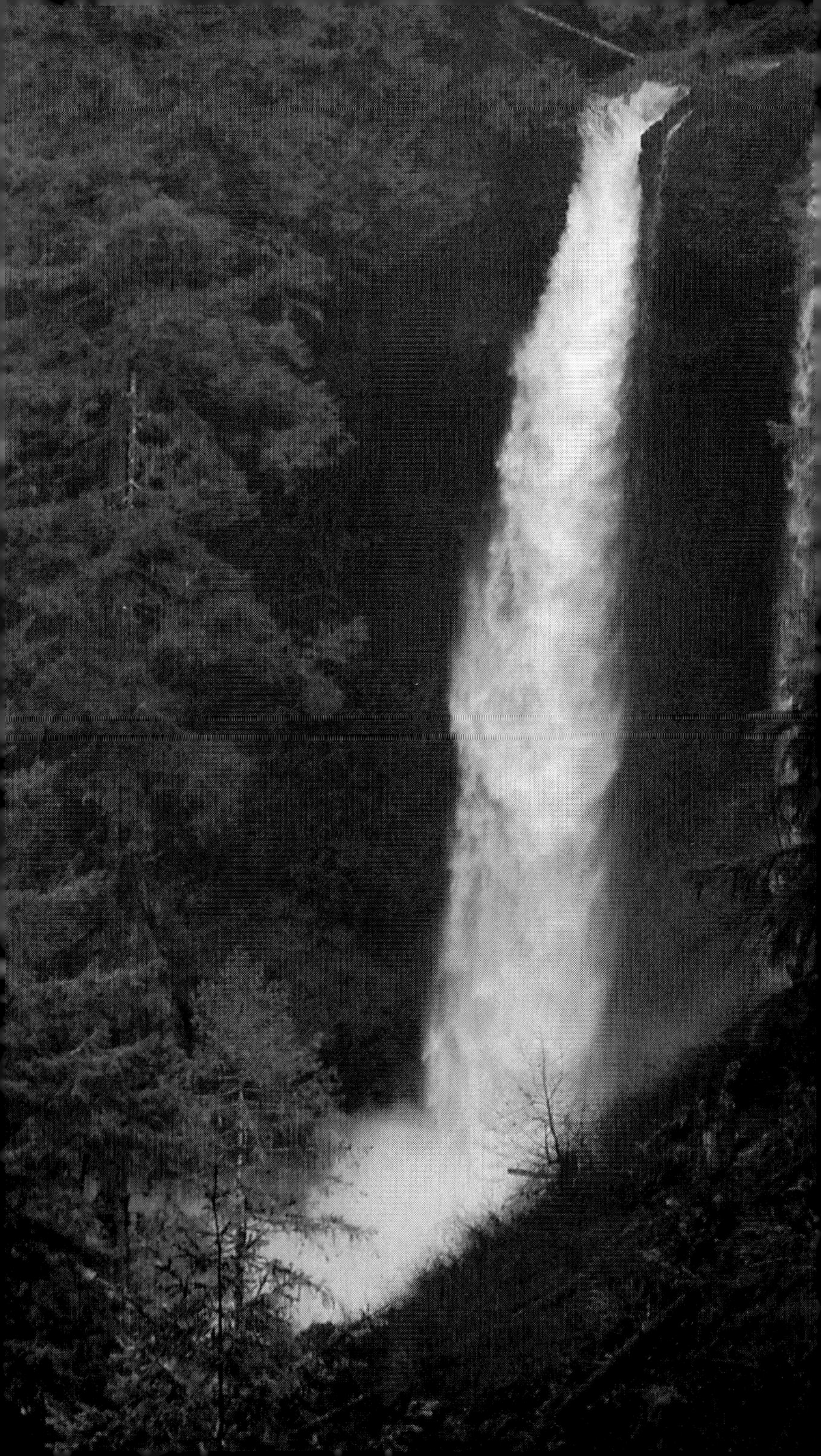

I'm Going on a Cruise

The church service had ended. In front of me was an older lady I had seen many times before. She was talking with a friend. I overheard her say:

"The doctor said it was malignant. He wants me to come in tomorrow. He is going to do more tests. I need to decide what I want to do."

I hung back as they finished their conversation and then approached her:

"Would you like me to pray over you?" I felt prompted to ask, but I didn't expect a positive answer. We had seen one another in church, but weren't well acquainted.

"Well, yes. Yes, I would."

"Not here."

"Why don't you follow me to my house," she answered.

I agreed. When we got there I instructed her:

"It is better if you lay down. I find people tend to fall asleep when I pray over them."

"Oh, that would be fine." She could see I was a bit nervous, so she said,

"I believe in healings, you know."

"You do?"

I was surprised at her forthrightness.

"Yes. When I was a little girl my sister was in a wheelchair. A man came to town and prayed over her. After that she could walk, so I believe in healings." She broke out in a big smile over this memorable moment in her life as she led me to her bedroom.

She has more faith than I do, I thought as I followed her. I was new at this.

She laid down and I sat beside her on the bed. I found talking out loud difficult, so I said to her:

"I prefer to pray silently."

Silence allows me to listen for the Lord's instructions.

"That's fine. I'll be praying too."

She pointed to the infected kidney where the doctor had detected a tumor. I placed one hand there and began to pray. Usually when I pray I feel a great amount of heat, but this time was different. I wondered if anything was happening.

Where is the Water?

After about 20 minutes she fell asleep. I quietly stood up, found my way to the front door and let myself out. Two weeks later I saw her sitting a few rows in front of me at church. When she got up to leave she spotted me. She smiled as she approached:

"How are you doing?" I asked her.

"I'm fine. I'm going on a cruise!"

That was far from the answer I expected. She continued:

"After you prayed over me I went to the doctor. He thought he was going to tell me he was going to have to operate, so he did some more preliminary tests. When he called me back he said he could not find the tumor. He knows it was there because he had pictures of it, but when he took more tests he could not find any evidence of it."

"That's wonderful!" I was so surprised.

"I told you I believe in healings. The Lord healed me. I'm going on a cruise!" Her eyes were bright and dancing with excitement.

About two years later we were getting ready to move. I saw her in church again and asked:

"How are you doing?"

With the same bright eyes and smile she said, "Fine, just fine," and then all excited she added, "I'm going on another cruise!"

In Reflection

The Lord could have asked someone else to pray over her. It amazes me how he can work through me even when I am hesitant and lacking confidence. Over and over again he teaches me that it is not about my ability, it is about his compassion and power.

The Challenge

Going forward with a mustard seed of faith takes trust in God, humility and courage. Believe he gives the means to accomplish what he asks you to do.

Look not to your own strength, abilities or wisdom. Instead stay focused on God. Cultivate an ear to hear him. Be confident that he knows exactly when and how to accomplish each goal.

What do you believe God is inviting you to do? How will you step out in faith and follow his command?

Remember you are not going alone. Like a beautiful dance, he will lead. All you have to do is stay tune to his promptings and take it one step at a time.

∞ **Further Study** ∞

"Come and see the works of God, Who is awesome in His deeds toward the sons of men. He turned the sea into dry land; they passed through the river on foot..."

Psalm 66:5-6

"They will see the glory of the LORD, The majesty of our God. Encourage the exhausted, and strengthen the feeble....' Then the eyes of the blind will be opened, And the ears of the deaf will be unstopped... For waters will break forth in the wilderness..."

Isaiah 35:2-6

"Let your light shine before men in such a way that they may see your good works, and glorify your Father who is in heaven."

Matthew 5:16

"But the Master said, 'You don't need more faith. There is no 'more' or 'less' in faith. If you have a kernel of faith, say the size of a poppy seed, you would say to this sycamore tree, 'Go jump in the lake,' and it would do it.'"

Luke 17:6

I'm Going On a Cruise

"When I was a child, I used to speak as a child, think as a child, reason as a child; when I became a man, I did away with childish things. For now we see in a mirror dimly...and I shall know fully just as I also have been fully known. But now abide faith, hope, love, these three; but the greatest of these is love."

I Corinthians 13:11-13

"What marvelous love the Father has extended to us! Just look at it—we're called children of God! That's who we really are. But that's also why the world doesn't recognize us or take us seriously, because it has no idea who he is or what he's up to."

1 John 3:1

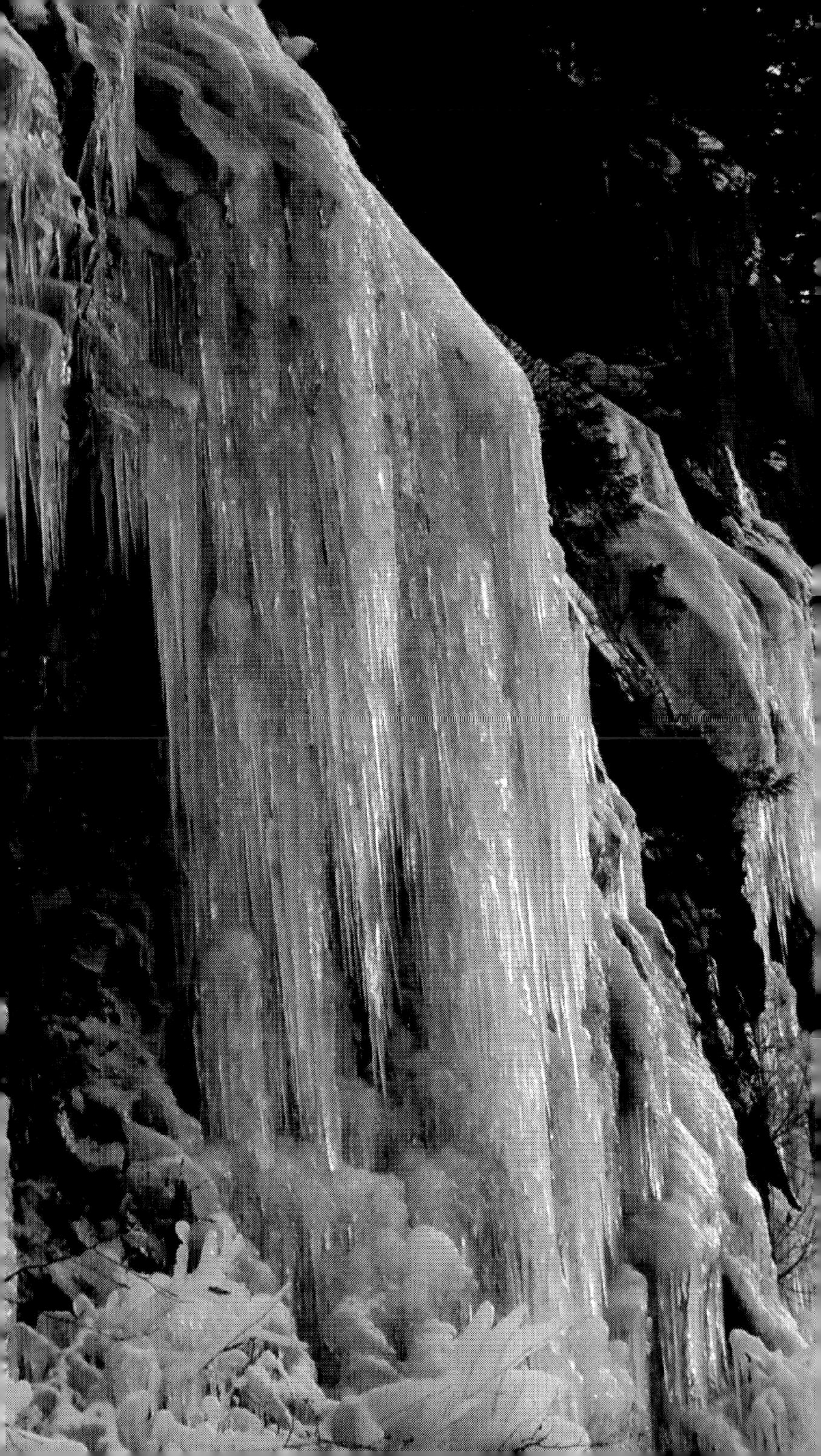

If You Wait
It Will Be Too Late

Hospitals are not one of my favorite places to be, but I felt prompted to pray with a friend whose dad was in the Intensive Care Unit. I wondered, as the elevator vibrated its way up to ICU, if the hospital staff would stop me from visiting. I was not a family member.

When I exited the elevator and rounded the corner I spotted my friend sitting on a bench outside her father's room. She was with another woman from church. I addressed the lady from church:

"I didn't know you were going to be here."

"I had to come into town, so I thought I'd spend a few minutes visiting."

We all chatted for awhile; it seemed to me everything was under control.

Perhaps I didn't need to come. I knew the lady from church would pray with my friend. After about ten minutes I said goodbye and left.

If You Wait It Will Be Too Late

It was lunch time when I got home. I fixed a plate of food and then sat down in my favorite rocking chair. The mid-afternoon sun was streaming through the trees outside. Its warmth found its way to me while I ate and prayed. I asked the Lord to watch over my friend and her father. Within me the Lord spoke:

"I want you to go back down to the hospital after lunch."

I argued, *"I made plans to go back tomorrow. She has a doctor's appointment in the city, but when she gets back she is going to call me. I'll pray with her then."*

"If you wait it will be too late. You need to go back today."

Too late? I thought to myself. *What does that mean?*

Through many experiences I've learned not to argue. I cleaned up my dishes and headed for the hospital. When I got there my friend was laying on a cot beside her Dad.

"Are you alright?" I inquired.

"My jaw hurts. I'm just a little tired."

She was going to the city the next day to have her jaw looked at.

"Would you like me to pray over your jaw?"

"Sure." She did not hesitate.

Where is the Water?

I carefully placed my right hand on her jaw and began to silently pray. She placed her hand over mine. I could feel warmth go up my arm to my elbow. I opened my eyes and looked at her in surprise.

"I have that gift too," she smiled at me.

"I didn't know."

"I didn't know you had it," she echoed. "I mostly pray over babies, because no one knows and they aren't going to tell anyone."

"Me too!"

We instantly connected. I asked her,

"Do you want me to pray over your dad with you? I came back, because I believe that is what I am supposed to do."

"Sure," she got up and went over to the other side of her father's bed.

He opened his eyes and looked at her. His expression showed his fright and my heart went out to him. He had a respirator over his face. His arms were hooked up to what appeared to be dozens of tubes going every which way. I placed my hands on him and began to pray.

I could feel heat coming from my chest. It seemed to travel down my arms and out my hands. He must have felt it too, because he turned to look at me. His expression had softened. His big brown eyes no longer looked frightened. I had no idea what he was thinking, but very shortly he relaxed and drifted off to sleep. Thirty minutes later I was headed home.

The next afternoon my phone rang.

"I just got back from my appointment." It was my friend at the hospital. "Daddy died just before I got here. About 10 minutes ago. Don't bother coming. The rest of the family will be here soon."

As she talked the Lord's words from yesterday echoed in my head,

"If you wait it will be too late."

In Reflection

The lady from the church probably prayed with my friend. I thought it was enough. I still do not know why the Lord wanted me to pray with her and her father. But the fact was, he did. He knew time was running out. When I look back, I'm glad I obeyed and didn't stand in my own decision and argue. I can remember times when that was not true and I regret them.

Acting in obedience, without debating takes a long time to master; I still tend to argue first and respond later. It's a habit I find hard to break.

Where is the Water?

Fear of being wrong, of being embarrassed, disappointing God, stirring up others—they all seem like good reasons for not responding, but in the end the arguments don't hold water.

The Challenge

How about you? Is God asking you to step out and take a risk? If he is, don't wait too long. There are some things that have to be done now, because if you wait, the time to act will have passed.

Regret is a hard burden to bear. If you have regrets confess them before God. He forgives. Don't let past action dictate how you will respond today. Believe God forgives, loves and accepts you. Believe he wants you to reach out to others in his love.

What can you do to put the past behind you?

What decisions can you make today to act in obedience to God?

∞ Further Study ∞

"O LORD Almighty, blessed is the man who trusts in you."

Psalm 84:12

"Bless the LORD, you His angels, Mighty in strength, who perform His word, Obeying the voice of His word!"

Psalm 103:20

"We are destroying speculations and every lofty thing raised up against the knowledge of God, and we are taking every thought captive to the obedience of Christ, and we are ready to punish all disobedience, whenever your obedience is complete."

1 Corinthians 10:5

"...he became the source of eternal salvation for all who obey him and was designated by God to be high priest in the order of Melchizedek."

Hebrews 5:9-10

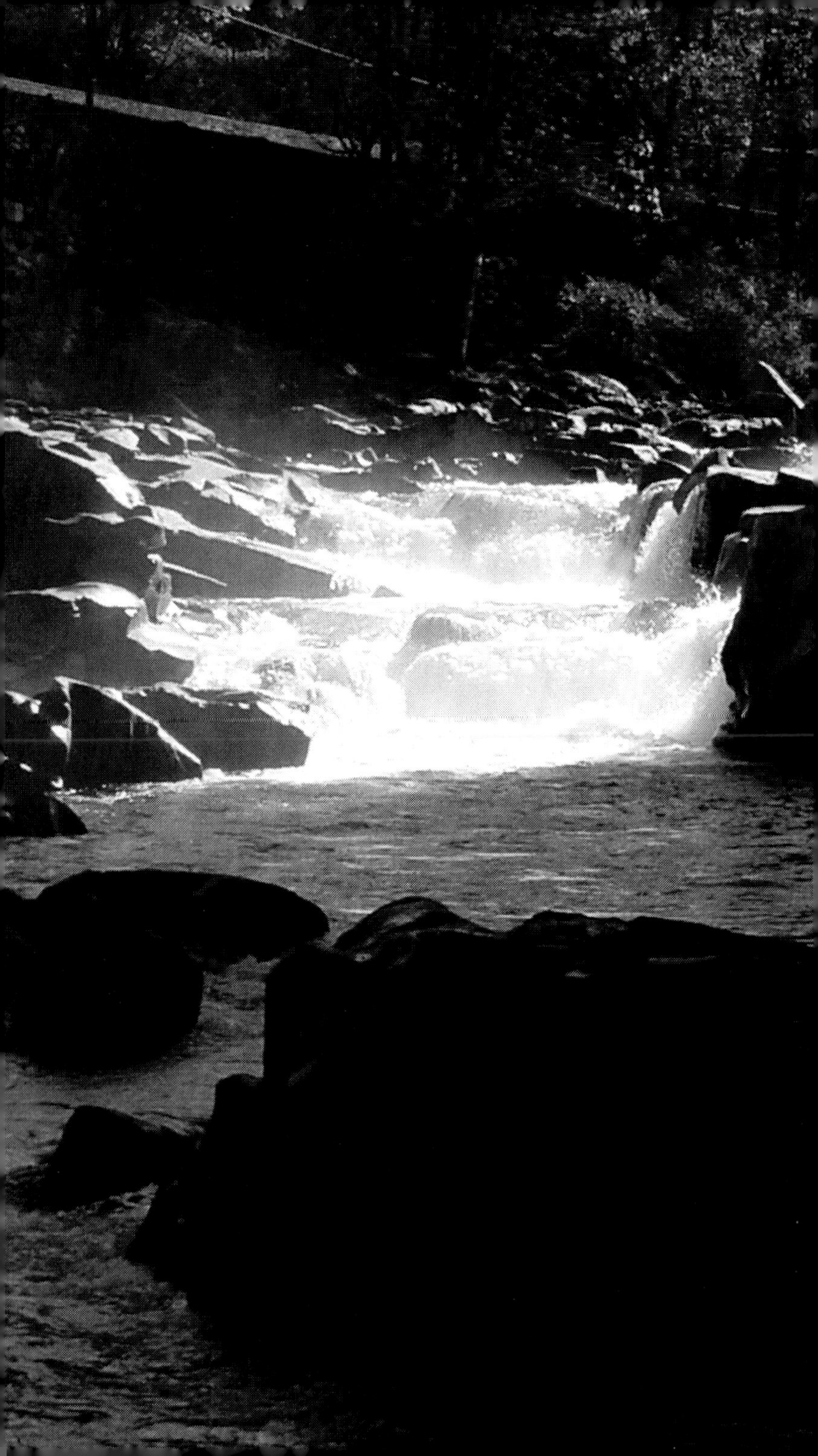

Do You Have a Few Minutes?

I had a meeting on campus. As usual I was early, so I decided to wait in the car and pray for awhile. I put the seat back and as I was settling in:

"*Go see Gerry. Show him what you are working on,*" the Lord's voice encouraged.

"*It's Friday. He won't be there. I have gone to this school long enough to know the Profs are not here on Friday.*"

"*Go check it out.*"

"*I don't have any of my material. I left my notebook at home. I've been up to his office on Friday's while I went to school here. He was never there.*"

There was silence. I tried settling in to pray. Silence.

"*Okay,*" I said reluctantly,

"*I've got an half hour. I'll walk over there.*"

I climbed the stairs to his office. To my surprise the door was open and he was sitting at his computer. I knocked on the door and he turned around:

Do You Have a Few Minutes?

"Do you have a few minutes?" I was a bit timid.

"I have twenty until I have to make a phone call."

"Can I show you something?"

"Come on in." He cleared the end of his desk to make room for me.

"I wanted to show you something. I tried to show it to you during a break we had in the Spiritual Warfare class I took from you last fall. It was not a good time, so I thought I'd show you now."

"What is it?"

I took a piece of scratch paper from his desktop and started to draw him the emotional wheel I had been working on. He seemed interested, so I pushed the conversation to deeper levels of ideas.

"I have read several books on lies. But I told the Lord:

'I can't remember all these lies. I'm never going to be able to write about them.'

When I send my husband to the store he says,

'If the list is longer than three items, you'd better write it down.'

Gerry nodded his head "yes" to let me know he was listening. I continued:

"I asked the Lord, 'Is there some way we can condense these lies?' He said,

'Diana, all lies are against the Trinity.' I thought, 'All lies are against the Trinity. That must mean there are three lies.'

But as I started working with them I realized there were four."

Gerry leaned forward, "Show me."

I showed him how the four lies were connected to the emotional wheel. He was writing down what I was saying.

I got so excited that he was actually listening to me that I could not remember the last lie. Our twenty minutes went by quickly and he said:

"When you get home email me that last lie; I'd like to know what it is."

"I'll do that!"

In Reflection

I don't remember who I was meeting on campus that day. I suspect Dr. Gerry Breshears was my "real" meeting. We met over the next two years as he reviewed and discussed my *Undivided Heart* books giving me encouragement, suggestions and helpful critiques.

As he says, "I saw the draft of the draft of the draft."

He was thrilled that I had taken an idea from one of his classes and developed it into two books. I had been gathering ideas for over 25 years, but his class helped me to formulate, process and label what I knew.

As I look back on that first meeting, I'm so glad I decided to put prayer into action, listen to the Lord and not just sit in my car!

The Challenge

The Lord knew all along I would need a theologian to help formulate my ideas and to endorse my book. He picked Gerry. I am so glad I listened to the Lord.

How about you? Is the Lord asking you to approach or work with someone that causes you to be timid, wary or apprehensive? Pray. Listen to the Lord's direction. Take a risk. He may have a divine appointment in mind. But you will never know unless you get up and go where he tells you.

∞ Further Study ∞

"And the LORD is the one who goes ahead of you; He will be with you. He will not fail you or forsake you. Do not fear, or be dismayed."

Deuteronomy 31:8

"Only be strong and very courageous; be careful to do according to all the law which Moses My servant commanded you; do not turn from it to the right or to the left, so that you may have success wherever you go."

Joshua 1:7

"Have I not commanded you? Be strong and courageous! Do not tremble or be dismayed, for the LORD your God is with you wherever you go."

Joshua 1:9

"The counsel of the LORD stands forever, The plans of His heart from generation to generation."

Psalm 33:11

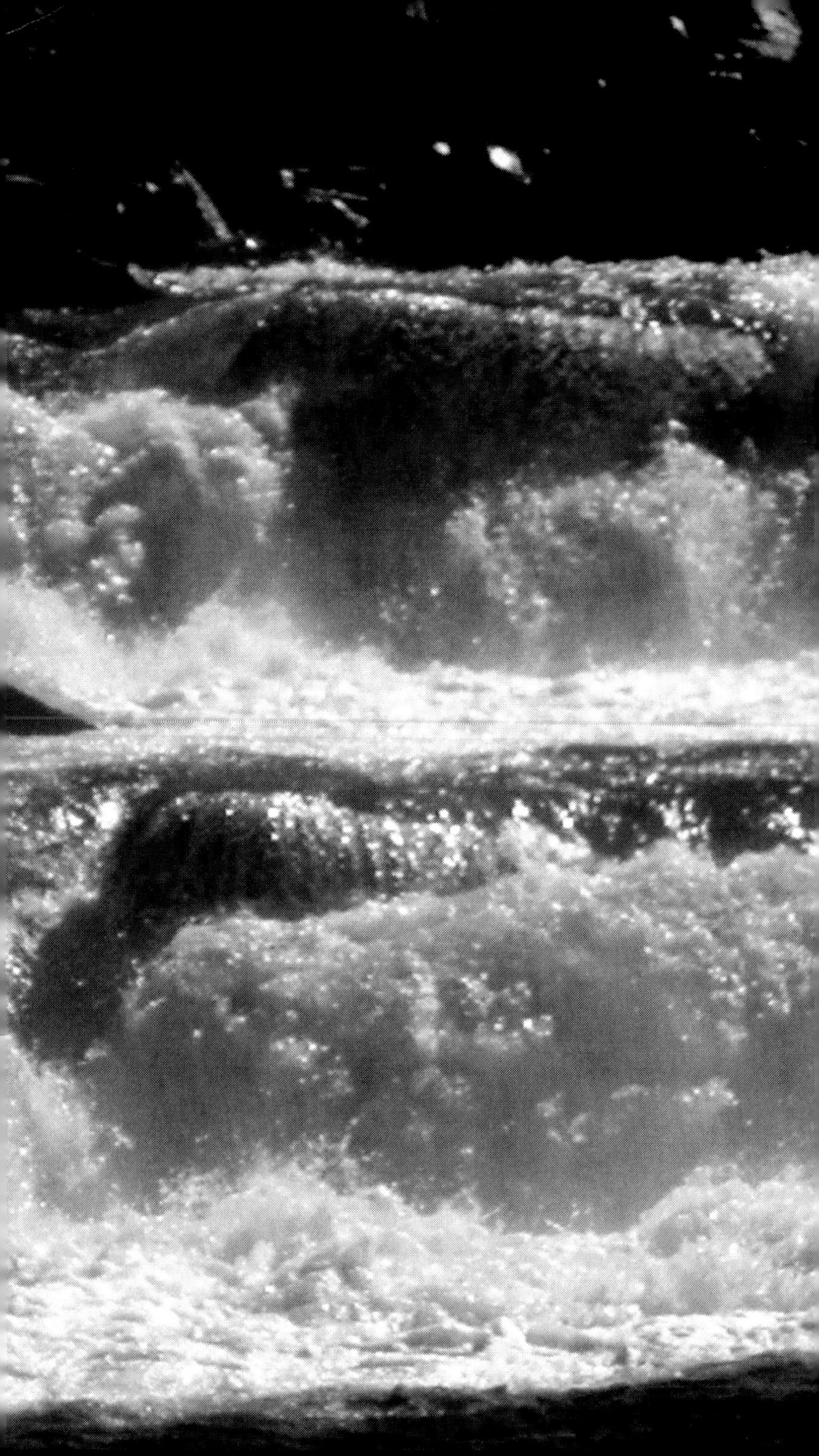

You Can Go Deeper

In my senior year of college I took a psychology course. It was a typical early 70's psych class. Instead of desks we used large stair steps covered with light green shag carpeting. Overly stuffed pillows strategically placed around the room gave a homey, comfortable atmosphere.

The class was pass/fail, which meant participation was key to doing well. This was no problem since I loved to talk. From the very beginning the 35 to 40 students in the class were broken down into smaller groups. We were expected to meet outside the classroom in individuals' homes or apartments, along with our weekly meetings in the shag carpet room. My small group "gelled" quickly and I enjoyed it.

The last day of class we met in the classroom. The professor instructed us to line each other up according to who we believed grew the most in understanding and knowledge of themselves during the quarter.

Without exception everyone positioned me at the head of the line. Before I had a chance to consider anyone's place in line the instructor asked his teaching assistant to put us in the order he thought we belonged. When he placed me last there was a low murmur in the room.

"No one seems to agree with him," the Prof was addressing me. "Do you agree with him, Diana? Or do you think he is wrong?"

I hung my head and stared at the floor. The teacher was standing in front of me now.

"Diana, do you belong in this spot or not?"

"Yes," I said quietly.

"What did you say? We can't hear you?"

Without looking up I said, "Yes, I belong here."

There was a distinct buzz of confusion in the room as everyone started whispering.

"Do you want to explain to everyone why you belong here—last in line?"

I shook my head "no."

"No?" He queried. Then suddenly he swung around and faced the group that had formed a semicircle around us.

"No!" He dramatically repeated addressing his audience. "You see, all this quarter Diana had been sharing with us deep insights into herself. She dazzled us with her newfound revelations, but the truth is…"

He turned to face me again and said, "The truth is she did not share anything of herself that she did not already intimately know."

I could feel my face hot with embarrassment.

Facing the group he continued, "She made us believe that, like you, she was learning new profound insights."

He had the group's attention.

"But she lied to you."

He pivoted back around and came into my space, "You cheated us and you cheated yourself!"

He dramatically turned back to his audience emphasizing his speech with spread out arms. I could no longer hear him. But I could see he was making his point to the group. And then he spun around to face me again only this time he came within an inch of my nose, looked straight into my eyes and said,

"I tell you, 'You can go deeper.'"

In Reflection

It seems that whenever I am tempted to plateau—to say, "I have grown enough. It is enough, because no one understands me now. Why should I grow anymore?" The Lord brings this incident back to my memory and says,

"You can go deeper."

Sometimes I feel like a gifted and talented child that cannot seem to find the language to speak to others about the insights they are discovering.

I understand these children because like them I often feel alone, deserted and misunderstood. I watch these children—how they cope, how they attempt to fit in by denying the gifts the Lord has given them.

And then I observe other children who choose instead to reach out, to share, to try and find a way to communicate what they are learning. They encourage me not to give up, but to ask in humility,

"Lord, how can I connect the concepts you have shown me? What do you want me to do?"

Through this college incident many years ago the Lord reminds me,

"Share the revelations and the truth I have given you. I will show you how."

I know I am not to cheat myself or others of the gifts he has given, but sometimes I'd rather hide.

The Challenge

Has the Lord given you insights or gifts that you are meant to share with others? Are you afraid others will not understand?

Where is the Water?

Are you afraid of rejection? God asks you to trust him, to come before him in humility and let him lead the way.

You may be a "nobody" like Abram, Moses, Ruth, Rahab, David, Mary and Saul in Scripture, but God calls you into his family. You may feel you are not quite good enough or eloquent enough. God promises to give you the wisdom and power that you need to overcome any obstacle within or outside yourself.

The truth is you are loved, you belong, and in humility you can be who God is calling you to be.

What fear do you need to overcome in order to step forward for God?

Where can you begin to share your gifts, your talents that the Lord has given you?

When will you pray and ask for his help? How will you go about making God's dreams for you a reality?

∞ Further Study ∞

"'Take off your sandals, for the place where you are standing is holy ground' ... 'Who am I, that I should go to Pharaoh and bring the Israelites out of Egypt?'... 'I will be with you.' 'What if they do not believe me?' ... 'This,' said the LORD, 'is so that they may believe that the LORD, the God of their fathers—the God of Abraham, the God of Isaac and the God of Jacob—has appeared to you.' ... 'I have never been eloquent...I am slow of speech and tongue' ... 'I will help you speak and will teach you what to say.'"

Exodus 3:5, 11, 12; Ex 4:1, 10, 12

"The righteous cry out, and the LORD hears them; he delivers them from all their troubles. The LORD is close to the brokenhearted and saves those who are crushed in spirit."

Psalm 34:17-18

"Trust GOD from the bottom of your heart; don't try to figure out everything on your own. Listen for GOD's voice in everything you do, everywhere you go; he's the one who will keep you on track. Don't assume that you know it all. Run to GOD! Run from evil!"

Proverbs 3:5-12

Where is the Water?

"Don't let the wise brag of their wisdom. Don't let heroes brag of their exploits. Don't let the rich brag of their riches. If you brag, brag of this and this only: that you understand and know me. I'm GOD, and I act in loyal love."

Jeremiah 9:23-24

"Do you not know that you are a temple of God, and that the Spirit of God dwells in you? ... Let no man deceive himself. If any man among you thinks that he is wise in this age, let him become foolish that he may become wise."

1 Corinthians 3:16, 18

"... grow in the grace and knowledge of our Lord and Savior Jesus Christ. To Him be the glory, both now and to the day of eternity. Amen."

1 Peter 3:18

Where is the Water?

The digital clock slowly advanced as I sat eating breakfast one morning. I was not focused on any particular thought when I heard:

"Do you get it yet?"

"Get what?" I questioned.

"Where is the water? Did you figure it out?"

"What do you mean? I don't understand."

"Have you answered the question?"

The Lord was referring to a song I had written called *Where is the Water?* Like a DVD playing in my mind, I could see myself and the events that brought the inspiration for that song.

∞∞∞∞∞∞∞

Dialogue: Where is the Water?

It was a hot summer day. John was cutting firewood and I was taking a jug of water out to him. As I crossed the dry streambed on our property, I was thinking about how sultry it was and how hard John was working. At that moment a slight breeze touched my cheek and brushed a wisp of hair out of my eyes and then was gone. I started to sing what I was feeling:

> "It's hot and it's dry and I thirst for You.
> Where is the shade and the breeze from You?
> Where is the water I need to survive?
> Where is the joy you said would be mine?"

The song was a lament on how the Lord made promises of joy and peace, but I was failing to see those promises fulfilled in my life. Instead life was stressful.

The voice within me brought me back to the present,

"You have been writing stories about your life. You tell your students to reflect on their life from the day before. You have been reflecting back on the years of your life."

Like a DVD playing in vivid color some of those stories flashed through my mind:

  -a teenage girl with a razor blade at my neck
  -a delivery truck rolling down a hill at me

Where is the Water?

-my two and half year old son learning to breathe while swimming

-my five-year-old wanting to pray and ask Jesus for protection

the faces of people I prayed for all came back to me.

As I watched the stories of my life, the voice continued:

"Do you understand where the water is now? In each story it was an ordinary day, until the power of the Holy Spirit touched it."

"I understand that the water is the water of the Holy Spirit," I said in answer.

"You have been stepping back and seeing the thread running through your life."

Realization was coming to me—the thread running through my life was prayer. God was there. The water of life came in the ordinary moments of my day. While I was doing mundane things the Lord reached out and touched my life just like he did the woman at the well. (John 4:5-42)

The Holy Spirit involved himself in the ordinary events of my life just like he did Mary's; a lowly peasant girl, who was open to doing God's will. It's an incredible story. I am just now getting it—a baby born to a peasant woman, an ordinary event that became extraordinary because she said, "Yes" to the involvement of the Holy Spirit in her life.

I was being shown how life is full of little

Dialogue: Where is the Water?

stories and the *"streams of living water,"* the Holy Spirit, flowed through each one of them. If I was willing to keep my eyes and ears open I would continue to see and hear the extraordinary in the midst of the ordinary.

In Reflection

In reaction to my life lived in the Lord, some people say to me:

"You think you have God in your pocket."

On the contrary, I don't tell God what to do, he tells me. He has me in his pocket. I surrender and obey as he fulfills his promises and plans, not mine.

Some people say to me:

"You've had experiences none of the rest of us have had."

In reality many people throughout history have had similar experiences. The Bible and the saints' autobiographies are full of such stories. An extraordinary life is available to you when you are willing to surrender, willing to listen and willing to see God in your everyday life.

For instance, you and I may have similar experiences. What makes the difference is our perception of those events.

Where is the Water?

When you view your life through the eyes and ears of the Holy Spirit your sanctified life in Christ makes the difference in your spiritual sight.

Others have said to me:

"You think you have a hotline to God."

The fact is he breaks into my world. When he arrives it is an ordinary day, nothing special about it. He chooses the time and the place. I have made myself available.

The Challenge

The stories in *Where is the Water?* happened to ordinary people, on an ordinary day, going about their ordinary business *until the extraordinary happened.*

The Holy Spirit reaches out when you least expect him. How can you train yourself to hear his voice, to see his wondrous deeds happening all around you and *walk with him all day long?*

My hope is that through the stories in this book you will hear and see your own life differently and you will be alert to find God in your every day experiences.

There is nothing like discovering the secret of turning an ordinary day into an extraordinary one.

Dialogue: Where is the Water?

I pray you become more aware of the love of God that surrounds you and flows from within you like—
"streams of living water."

∞ Further Study ∞

"For I will pour out water on the thirsty land and streams on the dry ground; I will pour out My Spirit on your offspring and My blessings on your descendants; and they will spring up among the grass like poplars by streams of water."

Isaiah 44:3-4

"Hey there! All who are thirsty, come to the water! Are you penniless? Come anyway—buy and eat! ...Listen to me, listen well: Eat only the best, fill yourself with only the finest. Pay attention...listen carefully to my life—giving, life nourishing words."

Isaiah 55:1-2

"I will always show you where to go. I'll give you a full life in the emptiest of places—firm muscles, strong bones. You'll be like a well-watered garden, a gurgling spring that never runs dry."

Isaiah 58:11

Where is the Water?

"Arise, shine; for your light has come, And the glory of the LORD has risen upon you. For behold, darkness will cover the earth, And deep darkness the peoples; But the LORD will rise upon you, And His glory will appear upon you."

Isaiah 60:1-2

"The Spirit of the LORD GOD is upon me, Because the LORD has anointed me To bring good news to the afflicted; He has sent me to bind up the brokenhearted, To proclaim liberty to captives, And freedom to prisoners…"

Isaiah 61:1

"…but whoever drinks of the water that I shall give him shall never thirst; but the water that I shall give him shall become in him a well of water springing up to eternal life."

John 4:5

"Whoever believes in me, as the Scripture has said, streams of living water will flow from within him."

John 7:38

"Awake, sleeper, and arise from the dead, and Christ will shine on you."

Ephesians 5:14

Dialogue: Where is the Water?

"Here I am! I stand at the door and knock. If anyone hears my voice and opens the door, I will come in and eat with him, and he with me. To him who overcomes, I will give the right to sit with me on my throne, just as I overcame and sat down with my Father on his throne. He who has an ear, let him hear what the Spirit says to the churches."

Revelations 3:20-22

"Come!" say the Spirit and the Bride. Whoever hears, echo, "Come!" Is anyone thirsty? Come! All who will, come and drink, Drink freely of the Water of Life!"

Revelations 22:17

Where is the Water?

It's hot and it's dry and I thirst for You,
Where is the shade and the breeze from You?
Where is the water I need to survive?
Where is the joy you said would be mine?

I can't see You, You're nowhere around.
I can't see You, You can't be found.
I'm searching and searching, but where are You?
I'm searching and searching, but I can't find You.

I work and I work all day for You,
I'm building and building all day for You.
So, where is the water I need to survive?
Where is the Peace ... You promised me?

I'm thirsting and thirsting, I need You now.
I'm thirsting and thirsting, I don't care how.
Oh, where is the water I need to survive?
Oh, where is the water, oh, please don't hide.

So, where is the water I need to survive?
Where is the Hope I need to stay alive?
Oh, where is the Promise, You made to me?
Has it all died on Calvary?

I know in my Heart, You're still there,
I know in my Heart that You still care.
But, where is the water I need to survive?
Oh, where is the water, oh, please don't hide.

Lord, Lord, where are You?
Lord, Lord, I can't find You.
Lord, Lord, I can't see,
Lord, Lord, please help me!

Where is the water? I need to survive,
Where is the water? I need to stay alive.
Oh, where is the water? I need to survive,
Where is the water?— I need to stay alive!

Diana E. Greene
© July 1985

SUGGESTED RESOURCES FOR GROWTH

Ruth Haley Barton (2006), *Sacred Rhythms, Arranging Our Lives for Spiritual Transformation*, Downder Grove, IL, InterVarsity Press

Oswald Chambers (1935, renewed 1963) *My Utmost for His Highest*, Westwood, NJ, Barbour and Company, Inc

Larry Crabb (1999), *The Safest Place on Earth*, Nashville, TN, W Publishing Group, A Division of Thomas Nelson, Inc

Mark Driscoll and Gerry Breshears (2008), *Death by Love: Letters from the Cross,* Wheaton, Il, Crossway books, a publishing ministry of Good News Publishers

Diana E. Greene (2010), *Undivided Heart, Book One and Book Two, Bridging My Relationship with Myself, Others and God*, Molalla, OR, Diana Greene Ministries, LLC

Sara Groves, *Precious Again*

Jeremy Hall (2007), *Silence, Solitude, Simplicity*, Collegeville, MN, Liturgical Press

Beverly White Hislop (2003), *Shepherding a Woman's Heart*, Chicago, Il, Moody Publishers

Max Luxado (2009), *FEARLESS, Imagine Your Life Without Fear*, Nashville, TN, Thomas Nelson

Ralph Martin (2006), *The Fulfillment of All Desire,* Stenbenville, OH, Emmaus Road Publishing

Brennan Manning (2002), *Ruthless Trust, The Ragamuffins, Path to God, New York, NY* Harper Collins Publications, Inc

John Ortberg (2002), *The Life You've Always Wanted,* Grand Rapids, Michigan, Zondervan

Jill Phillips (2003) *Writing on the Wall,* Fervent Records

John Piper (2000), *Pleasures of God, Meditations on God's Delight in Being God,* Sisters, OR, Mulnomah Publishers, Inc

Michael John Poirier (1992) *Oceans of Mercy,* Franklin Park, Il, Prayersongs Publishing Company

Judy Squier (2010), *His Majesty in Brokenness,* Grants Pass, OR Judy Squier Ministries

Charles R. Swindoll (1993), *Flying Closer to the Flame, A Passion for the Holy Spirit,* Dallas, London, Vancouver, Melborne, Word Publishing

Ann Voskamp, (2010), *One Thousand Gifts: Dare to Live Fully Right Where You Are*, Grand Rapids, Michigan Zondervan

Bruce Wilkinson (2003), *The Dream Giver,* Sisters, OR, Multnomah Publishing

Want an Intimate Relationship with God?

Where is the Water? invites you to train yourself to hear God's voice and open your eyes to his presence. He desires to be known. He longs to share his love. Acquire renewed faith, hope and confidence that God can and will transform your ordinary days into extraordinary ones.

Undivided Heart - Book One
Bridging My Relationship with Myself, Others and God

Discover the personal stories or events in your life that have you stuck emotionally and spiritually. Expose the four lies that hold you back from an intimate relationship with God. Gain a new perspective. Take action. Equip yourself with eight truths. Risk to live a new life filled with joy!

Undivided Heart - Book Two
Bridging My Relationship with Myself, Others and God

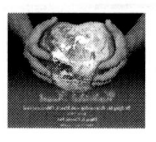

Learn the five levels of communication that enhance or hinder your relationships. Let God heal the wounds of your soul caused by betrayal, humiliation, abandonment or alienation. Gain the power that enables you to love yourself and others.

For books, blog, or to schedule Diana Greene to speak at a conference, retreat or seminar, please visit www.dianagreeneministries.com.

Diana Greene Ministries, LLC PO Box 902, Molalla, OR 97038

Praise for *Undivided Heart, Books One and Two*

"Diana's love for Jesus and long journey of a deep personal walk with Him gave her the wealth of experience to integrate many facets of spiritual formation into a course of study and a work book that enables people to find what divides their hearts, minds and emotions."

Gerry Breshears, PhD
Professor of Theology
Western Seminary, Portland, OR
Co-Author of *Death by Love*

"I found the manuscript to be inspired by the Holy Spirit and done in excellence. I believe it will inspire those who are blessed to participate in her teaching. I was certainly encouraged when I read it. It is so timely and introspective. It promotes personal growth and healing in emotions, as one experiences the heart of God."

Virginia Phillips, PhD
Founder & President, Women of Purpose, International
Author of *Heart to Heart Connection*

"Through scripture Diana taught us how to move from fear to courage, from confusion to peace, from a feeling of being unloved to acceptance, from hopelessness and depression to joy & fulfillment. I was able to identify the lies I believed and begin renewing my mind with the truth of God's Word. I strongly recommend the class. It will change your life as it has changed mine."

Barbara Baker
Mother, grandmother
Office worker
Pastor's wife

Where is the Water? can enhance your: personal devotions, Bible study, small group discussions and retreats or seminars. The Challenge and Further Study following each story encourage you and others to develop an intimate prayer life with God.

For books, blog, or to schedule Diana Greene to speak at a conference, retreat or seminar, please visit www.dianagreeneministries.com.

Diana Greene Ministries, LLC PO Box 902, Molalla, OR 97038

137 - Water = ordinary moments of the day.
prayer = thread running thro' life.